MOTIVATIONAL INTERVIEWING WORKBOOK

WORKSHEETS, ACTIVITIES & DESK REFERENCES FOR THERAPISTS

BASIC SUMMARY OF THE APPROACH
STAGES OF CHANGE
S.M.A.R.T GOAL SETTING & VALUE EXPLORATION
READINESS RULER...

...AND OTHER WORKSHEETS & FLOW CHARTS DESIGNED TO SUPPORT YOUR MOTIVATIONAL INTERVIEWING APPROACH

MOTIVATIONAL INTERVIEWING:

THE BASICS

"

If you wish to
know the mind
of a man, listen
to his words...

"

JOHANN WOLFGANG VON
GOETHE

Copyright 2023- All rights reserved.

The information in this book is based on the author's knowledge, experience, and opinions. The methods described in this book are not intended to be a definitive set of instructions. You may discover other methods and materials to accomplish the same result. Your results may differ. This book is presented for informational and entertainment purposes only.

The information is provided "as is," to be used at your own risk. Under no circumstances will any legal responsibility or blame be held against the publisher or author for any reparation, damages, or monetary loss due to the information herein, either directly or indirectly. This book is not intended to give health or medical advice and is sold with the understanding that the author is not engaged in rendering professional services or advice. Again, the intent is to offer readers information of a general nature and for entertainment purpose only. In the event you use any of the information or sheets found in this book for yourself or for a client, the author and publisher assume no responsibility for such actions.

Copyright © 2023. Book is intended for personal use; Commercial use is not allowed and is not for resale for any reason.

All Rights Reserved.

TABLE OF CONTENTS

Motivational Interviewing Workbook

DEDICATION

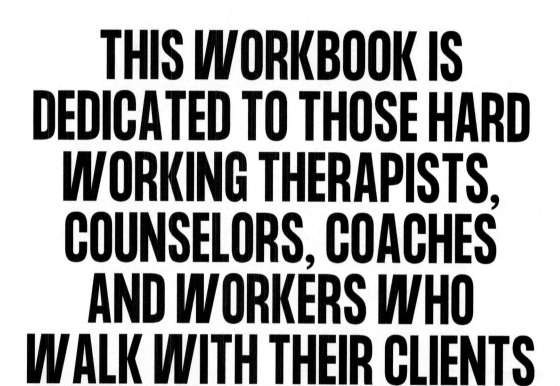

THIS WORKBOOK IS
DEDICATED TO THOSE HARD
WORKING THERAPISTS,
COUNSELORS, COACHES
AND WORKERS WHO
WALK WITH THEIR CLIENTS
TOWARDS A HEALTHY AND
BRIGHTER FUTURE

Synopsis of the Motivational Interviewing Approach

Famous American psychologist Carl Rogers, recognized mostly for his work in founding what is known best as Client-Centered Therapy or Rogerian Therapy, once stated how his approach to counseling worked: "*If I can provide a certain type of relationship, the other person will discover within himself the capacity to use that relationship for growth...and change and personal development will occur...*"

Here, Carl Rogers is speaking to the power of a client-centered counselor to serve as a support to their client on the path towards change. Notice he never claims to lead the client towards change through his expertise. Instead, he walks alongside his client on their personal journey as a teammate or collaborator. This allows the client to find their own agency, motivation and resource to make desired changes in their lives.

Having someone to walk with them is a true benefit, yet even with such support, creating sustainable life changes is not always easy! People can often find themselves split between their deep desires for change and the routine or comfort of familiar behaviors, even if those behaviors are causing the person distress. Maintaining the motivation for change can be tested.

This is where the groundbreaking work of psychologists William Miller and Stephen Rollnick can be of benefit. Miller and Rollnick are widely recognized in the mental health world as the founders of the therapeutic modality / approach known as Motivational Interviewing, or MI. This counseling approach is used in a variety of settings and for a lot of challenges, making it a fantastic and highly beneficial modality for therapists / counselors / teachers / coaches / social workers to learn as it can help many clients across many settings.

Anywhere there is a person considering change, MI can be there to support.

THE SPIRIT OF MOTIVATIONAL INTERVIEWING

Motivational Interviewing is practiced with an underlying set of principles that informs how the therapist aims to work with their clients. Such principles are often referred to as being the "spirit" of the approach. The spirit of MI is built upon an understanding that the approach is foundationally built upon the following ideals:

- **Partnership**: MI is a collaborative process between the therapist and the client. It is understood that the person is an expert in their lives and that the therapist can help them consider making changes in their life. The two will ideally work in tandem with each other along the journey.
- **Evocation**: The MI approach acknowledges that most people have within themselves many skills, resources and traits needed for change. It becomes a goal of the approach to help the client recognize these supportive factors while examining a person's personal values, experience, and motivations for considering a change to their status quo.
- **Acceptance**: Acceptance represents such an important foundational spirit of this approach to working with people. The MI therapist looks to maintain a nonjudgmental stance when working with their client. It is their intention to seek out a better understanding of their client's experiences - such will ultimately inform one's perspectives. Therapists look to build an authentic professional relationship while accepting that client's right to make the ultimate choices about changing behaviors or not changing. Autonomy is respected as is a client's capacity for self-direction.
- **Compassion**: Above all, there is always an ultimate care for the client. As said Miller & Rollnick in 2013, "Compassion is actions taken...benevolently to promote the client's welfare, giving priority to the client's needs."

Remember - It is ultimately the collaborative nature of the therapist-client relationship that is the main essence of MI, without which MI techniques will be ineffective.

Spirit of Motivational Interviewing [Diagram]

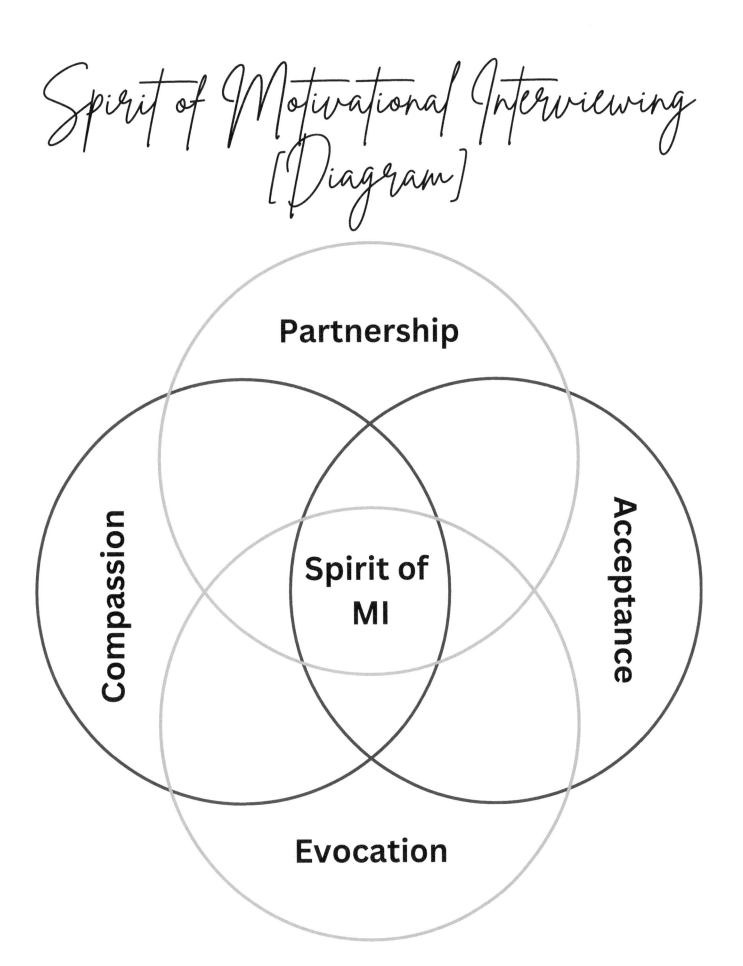

The Spirit of
Motivational Interviewing

Motivational interviewing (MI) is an effective tool and approach to counseling because it looks to enhance a person's motivation by working through any ambivalence. It requires a client to be able to recognize the true importance for change, their own resources and abilities to support the path towards change, and a sense of readiness to do the work. In other words, the client is ready, willing and able to change! The spirit of this approach requires partnership, collaboration, evocation, and acceptance of the client's autonomy. The table below is adapted from the work of Miller & Rollnick in 2002, which looked at the differences in tone/approach of MI and other more authoritative approaches:

Spirit of MI	Authoritative Approach
Collaboration, partnership and rapport between the therapist and client is formed. The therapist is not considered the sole expert in the room and decisions are made together. The therapist acknowledges the client's expertise about themselves.	An approach that looks to utilize confrontation rather than partnership: the therapist assumes their client has impaired view or perspective and presents needed 'insights.' Therapist may try and push a client towards change.
Evocation is key as the therapist activates their client's motivation for change by evoking their reasons for wanting / needing to change. The therapist looks to connect change to the things the client cares about and the values the client hold.	The client is presumed to lack some insight, ability or knowledge that is required for them to make change. Therapist takes on a more directive tone & approach in the relationship. Therapist is educating the client & the client is intended to follow that lead.
The client's autonomy is respected and accepted: although the therapist can inform and advise their client, they accept the client's freedom to decide NOT to change: 'It is ultimately up to you.'	The therapist instructs their client and looks to direct them towards making the changes. 'Here is what I want you to do.'

Why Motivational Interviewing Works

Motivational Interviewing is an empathetic yet powerful counseling approach that is designed to facilitate behavior changes by exploring and resolving roadblocks to change and growth. It explores ambivalence, stagnation, motivation, and that incredibly difficult feeling of "being stuck."

Most can relate to that feeling -- therapist and client alike.

MI is not a therapist-led clinical approach where clients are told what is wrong with them and what they need to do. Rather, at its core, MI is a collaboration between client and therapist that recognizes the complexities behind finding and maintaining the motivation for change.

The philosophy behind MI honors the personal autonomy of clients while examining and eliciting the motivations necessary for real change. It is not a "one size fits all" approach to working with someone and aims to meet them where they are at. Sometimes, a person does not recognize the real need for change even when others around them are pleading for it. Other times, a person can realize on a superficial level the need or want for something different but are stuck in the comfort that old habits bring. MI can meet them at whatever stage a person is at regarding their path towards change. There will be more on these different stages as we progress.

MI works because it understands that ambivalence and stagnation can be a natural part of the journey for most. Again, people often find themselves torn between the genuine desire for something new or different and the comfort of familiar behaviors, their status quo. Growth is not always a straight line forward. An easy example to conceptualize would be the husband who has gained significant weight as a result of poor nutritional habits and does not find the energy to workout.

He may think that his nutrition habits are acceptable. He may recognize that it would be fine to lose a pound or two. He may feel the need to make a plan toward change, but the habit of eating at the local fast food joint after work is too enticing...

Wherever a person is, the therapist armed with the MI mindset can meet them there.

This makes the style so important to learn as it allows a client the opportunity to explore any roadblocks without feeling judged openly. The style leads with empathy as the therapist adopts a non-confrontational stance while aiming to elicit more "change talk" from the client (statements that reflect a person's motivation, thoughts, commitment, and reasons for wanting change). Through active listening techniques such as reflective listening and strategic questioning, individuals can develop their own unique plans moving forward.

MI then looks to help a person plan for ways to move past ambivalence or feelings of being stuck. This client-centered process leads to a more robust, congruent commitment from the person and thus, a greater likelihood of sustainable change and growth. This is because it is THEM wanting to make a change, having spent quality time examining pros and cons, benefits and challenges in session.

THE 4 PROCESSES OF MOTIVATIONAL INTERVIEWING

The creators of MI, William Miller and Stephen Rollnick, describe the approach as *"a directive, client-centered counseling style for eliciting behavior change by helping clients to explore and resolve ambivalence."*

There are four essential processes of the motivational interviewing approach that are necessary for eliciting these changes.

The 4 Processes of Motivational Interviewing are:

- Engaging
- Focusing
- Evoking
- Planning

In Motivational Interviewing, these four processes are designed to build on each other while looking to invoke change. While this approach to counseling was designed for a therapeutic setting, it is amazing to consider how elements of MI can apply to so many walks of life. This makes sense: therapists and counselors aim to help their clients overcome mental & emotional challenge; coaches look to develop skills and build ideal habits in their players; teachers hope to encourage students to perform to their best in the classroom; parents aim to teach their children the skills required to be successful in life; business men and women aim to motivate their employees in working toward a common goal.

And it all begins by engaging.

Engaging
This aspect of the process would be familiar to anyone in the helping professions, as developing rapport with a client is the start for quality counseling and professional therapeutic alliance. Ideally, the therapist will foster a relationship that demonstrates the benefit of collaboration and trust. The importance of developing trust and confidence cannot be overstated. It is also important to remember that the process of engagement with a client is ongoing and is not something that only occurs in the first session and then is completed.

Understanding the importance of engagement, there are noteworthy considerations to remember along the way:
- To develop a genuine working relationship, the client needs to be able to trust their therapist.

- Therapists should focus on the person in front of them and remain present in the moment; avoid jumping into problem-solving mode too soon.
  - A common mistake within MI is troubleshooting problems before a client is ready for that step.
- Remember those foundational, active listening skills reviewed in most introductory graduate courses.
  - Focus on empathetic listening and reframing by giving the client full attention and care; the therapist should look to show that they are really listening attentively -- looking to understand rather than to find 'smart' or 'insightful' responses.
- Remember the importance of ideal metacommunication and nonverbals, e.g., simple head nods and open posture.

The therapist must also be aware of signs that a client is disengaged. If the client seems disengaged / disconnected by displaying any of the following 'red flag' warning signs, the therapist should consider returning to basic attending skills.

What would be signs that the client is not fully engaged?
- Giving short answers that seemed rushed or inauthentic.
- Closed-off body language; their metacommunication seems closed to you.
- Agreeing with you to move forward; inauthenticity.
- Silence or avoiding session.

A vital aspect to this process is utilizing "OARS" (The core skills of motivational interviewing include using **O**pen questions, **A**ffirmations, **R**eflections, and **S**ummaries). More on this as we progress. The next process to review is Focusing.

Focusing
Here, the therapist aims to help their client hone in on the 'nitty-gritty,' the area they struggle to change. The therapist will support their client in exploring any roadblocks that get in the way of making this change.

Focusing is an agreement between the therapist and the client that explicitly identifies the focus of their work together. This is a very important part of motivational interviewing because both parties agree on their shared focus and intention for sessions. This allows the therapist permission to move into a directional conversation about change in collaboration with their client without the client feeling like it is being forced on them.

From there, the therapist can always reiterate the collective focus throughout the conversations — all done while considering the importance of rapport, alliance, and engagement.

Maintaining focus is important for a therapeutic session. During an MI conversation, it is ideal to have a single focus, even though a person may be working through various challenges. When working with multi-faceted people, multiple focuses may come up during the natural flow of the dialogue. This is very common. Still, it is important to target a primary focus of the session. The area of focus should be clear, something within the client's power to control, and ultimately is something relevant to the client.

Without an identified target that the therapist/client tandem is focused on, a 'nice' conversation between them may occur...but it will be directionless and not aimed toward real change. During the overall process, a therapist looks to help guide the conversation - never entirely directing it nor simply 'going with it' without direction or purpose. If there was a continuum between 'Following' and "Leading' during a session, MI would be in the middle, 'guiding' or 'supporting' the process. They may sometimes lead and follow but try to avoid doing too much of either as it contradicts this particular modality and approach to counseling others.

Following ⟵⟶ **Guiding/Supporting** ⟵⟶ Leading

Evoking

An integral part of this entire process is being able to have a client openly consider any existing ambivalence and their reasons for and against making change. As has already been said, making the decision to change is not an easy one. The process of evoking means utilizing "change talk" to help the client thoroughly flush out their reasons for wanting change.

Why do they want to make this change?
Why are they motivated to do this work?

In this process, the therapist will help their client explore, ultimately building up their own "why" for making change. This will be done through the eliciting of ideas via thoughtful discussion. Any ambivalence encountered during this discussion is normalized as being part of the process (it is not considered to be a client trying to be 'difficult') and explored without judgment.

Evoking is an essential process to the MI approach because this conversation allows the therapist/client tandem to fully process the client's motivations, their resource, ability, and desire to make change. Therapists can explore this with their client, armed with open-ended questions and change talk. It is also a very important step to discuss any discrepancy between the client's desired goals and their current actions and behavior. Instead of telling someone what to do, MI looks to evoke the client's own motivation and resources for making change.

Discussing such matters openly may serve as a wonderful opportunity for a person as it may be the first time articulating their reasons for wanting to make a change. This demonstrates why the engagement phase and OARS are so important as having honest evoking-phase discussions would be challenging if a strong therapeutic relationship was not established via engagement.

Change is not always linear and the likelihood of struggle or "two steps forward, one step back" scenarios is almost expected in counseling from an MI mindset; the therapeutic relationship is the foundation upon which these steps forward or backward survive (and ultimately thrive).

Planning
If focusing is the "What" and evoking is the "Why," then planning is the "How."

Focusing identifies the target for discussion. Evoking helps a client make clear their reasons for change. Planning is the next step, determining how the client will take all their newly found insights and motivations and actually apply them. Here, they begin formulating a plan to move toward the desired change.

This step is important because a poorly formed plan will likely miss the mark.

Such makes plenty of sense. Planning anything of significance can be challenging for many people. Just having some motivation to improve is not enough; simply saying "I'm going to do it, I will quit smoking now" does not really formulate a worthy plan.

For example, it is common for a well-intentioned student to say that they want to "get good grades."

That sounds fine...but HOW? Is it possible to better define what it would mean to get better grades? What is the next small step to take toward the ultimate goal? The details of a good plan matter very much.

A skilled and attentive MI therapist will not settle there and they may look to help their client dig a little deeper. Of course, this would be done based on where they are in terms of relationship/rapport, the focus of the session and the insights uncovered.

"Digging Deeper" could include breaking the plan down into smaller steps, preparing for any potential roadblocks or "what if" scenarios, or even looking to get things off to a good start by identifying the next step in the process that can help the client succeed. Examining potential roadblocks can be incredibly important during this process so they can plan ahead and troubleshoot these barriers to success.

It is critical that the therapist always respects the timing and readiness of their client before diving into a plan.

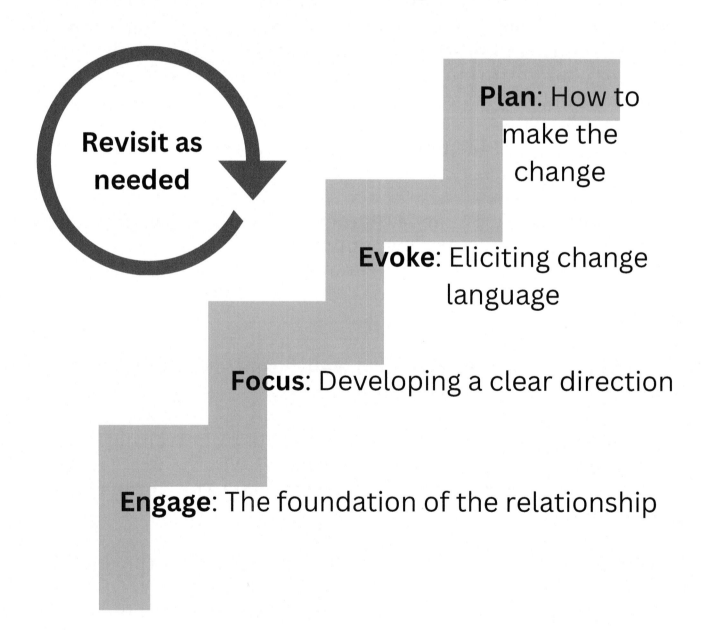

Revisit as needed

Plan: How to make the change

Evoke: Eliciting change language

Focus: Developing a clear direction

Engage: The foundation of the relationship

O.A.R.S As The Cornerstone

The **OARS** model is a cornerstone of the Motivational Interviewing approach created by Rollnick and Miller. OARS is a set of four key counseling skills that looks to develop rapport with a client, elicit important information through discussion, and ultimately enhance a client's motivation. OARS stands for **o**pen-ended questions, **a**ffirmations, **r**eflections and **s**ummaries. When these core skills are used, there will exist a greater chance to engage with clients, develop a solid professional relationship while also helping avoid confrontation and discord within the therapist-client relationship.

OARS is a foundational skill required if one is looking to utilize the MI approach to working with clients.

Open-Ended Questions
Using open-ended questions gives the client a chance to build trust and a professional relationship with the therapist while going into relevant details about their unique life story. Open-ended questions in motivational interviewing help facilitate key dialogue that requires more than a one word response or simple no or yes response:
- Open-ended questions usually begin with words or phrases like "how," "what," "can you describe to me" or "tell me more about," etc.
  - "Can you tell me more what you like about drinking?"
  - "What things would you like to be different?"

Affirmations
Affirmations look to acknowledge the client's resiliency, struggle and hard work both in and out of session. It is critical that when offering an affirmation, it be legitimate, congruent and honest as most people will be able to distinguish from a genuine affirmation and one that is said without congruence. When offering an affirmation, try and avoid coming off as being patronizing or over the top. As a rule of thumb, aways

mean what you say: if you are not genuine in your spoken affirmations, the client may recognize this lack of authenticity and their valuable trust may be lost or diminished. Some examples of affirmations could be:

- "You are a very strong person, emotionally resilient. You have shown that you can face down tough times."
- "You are a very descriptive speaker; I can visualize everything that you say."
- "I appreciate the conversation we had today, with you sharing so much and being so expressive and open."
- "I very much admire the work you put into being a good dad."

Reflections

Reflections and reflective listening skills are incredibly important when using a motivational interviewing approach to working with others. Reflections are used to show clients that you are listening to them attentively, allow the chance to show genuine interest and understanding in what the client is sharing.

Reflective listening and follow-up statements need to showcase the attentiveness of the therapist. Key factors to consider when offering reflective statements:

- The reflection offered by the therapist should avoid being longer than the original statement made by the client; if the therapist is doing more talking than the client, the reflection was not succinct enough and the therapist should think about what is causing this to be the case.
- Effective reflections can use words or phrases previously offered by the client as this demonstrates attentiveness and reflects the client's statements back to them, like a mirror.
- Reflections should look to examine the meaning of what a client has said; reflections can serve as a way for the therapist to ensure he/she understands what has been said by the client.

Summaries

Summarizing is an incredibly important tool within the MI framework and can be used throughout a session. Summaries, along with reflections, help a client hear back their own words, phrases and thoughts -- allowing them the chance to confirm their accuracy. Sometimes, when hearing a reflective statement or general summary stated back to them, a client may respond "no, no...that is not actually what I meant..."

Summaries can be a good, useful technique to assist the client in organizing their discussions in session, as well as their overall experience. For example, the therapist may look to reinforce what the client has said in session by using the following prompts:

- "If I am understanding you correctly, you are saying that..."
- "Tell me if I've missed anything here, but what I have heard you say is that..."
- "Let's take a second and make sure we are on the same page..."

The therapist should never assume that they have a full 100% grasp on the client's story and should always offer the chance for a client to amend previous statements or point out areas where the therapist's summary is incorrect/inaccurate:

- "Did I understand that correctly? Was there anything I missed?"
- "Did you want to add anything or correct any aspect of that summary?"
- "I really want to make sure I have a complete understanding of the timeline, so to review...did I cover everything?"

Open-Ended Q's	**Affirmations**
Q's that cannot be answered w/ Yes or No Invites the client to open and share; rely on active listening and genuine curiosity "Can you tell me more about...?" "What would happen next...?" "Clarify what you mean when you said..."	Authenticity and congruence is important; Therapist should aim to be sincere in recognizing the client successes or motivations "It says a lot about your care as a father that you are wanting to make this change..."
Reflections	**Summaries**
Offers the chance for therapist to show they are listening; helps create collaborative space Mirror what the client says in session "From what I hear you saying..." "It seems like..." "Wow, that must be..."	Further demo's to client that therapist is listening and understanding Tie together all relevant info into a concise summation; Client can hear back their story and responses, ambivalence and motivation "Ok, let me make sure I understand..."

KNOW THE R.U.L.E TO MOTIVATIONAL INTERVIEWING

When engaging in Motivational Interviewing, it is important to know the rules, or more importantly, the acronym RULE: **R**esist the righting reflect, **U**nderstand the client's motivations, **L**isten with empathy, and **E**mpower the client (Haque & D'Souza, 2019). Such are important principles to the method - critical reminders for the therapist to remember when working with their client.

Resist the Righting Reflex

The righting reflex is a desire or instinct on the part of the therapist to try and "fix" their client, to do the client's work for them while in session, or to try and correct their thoughts, feelings, or behaviors. Such a directive, authoritative style would be contrary to the MI approach. The therapist needs to foster a space that can allow their client to work through self-discovery. Without this, the client may just be doing what their therapist is telling them to do.

Understand the Client's Motivations

The therapist should be careful about assuming they fully understand the client's motivations too quickly. They should take the time to learn about their client while avoiding any assumptions.

Listen with Empathy

The therapist is responsible for fostering a space that is safe for the client to explore their thoughts and feelings without judgment. The therapist must practice quality active listening skills, showcase a genuine interest in the client's life and validate the client's experiences. If this is done well, they will be comfortable openly discussing change talk.

Empower the Client

For MI to be successful, the client must leave the therapeutic relationship with an understanding of their abilities, resources, and strengths. Knowing such will allow the client to understand the control they have over their own lives. They will be able to analyze whether their behaviors/actions are congruent with their values. The client will know that change is in their hands.

The Summation

Motivational interviewing (MI) is an empirical approach to counseling, a client-centered counseling style for eliciting change by helping people fully explore the reasons for wanting to change, resolve any ambivalence, and make plans on how to accomplish their established goals. The approach can be used across settings and situations, making it a versatile tool for a counselor's toolbelt.

MI has four fundamental processes that describe the general direction or "flow" of motivational interviewing with the understanding that movement back and forth between the processes is likely as change is often complex:
- Engaging: The foundation of MI looks to establish a professional alliance between the therapist and their client through attentive, active listening skills. This is considered an absolute foundational necessity for the MI approach.
- Focusing: The therapist and client move into a focused conversation about change, the "what" of MI.
- Evoking: The stage where a therapist works with their client in processing their own "why" for wanting to make the change. Any experienced ambivalence is understood to be part of the process, discussed, and explored without judgment.
- Planning: Planning explores the "how" of change - where the MI therapist supports their client in developing a plan based on that person's own personal life experience, insights, and general expertise. The client is considered the expert of their own life.

The approach can only work in an environment where there is an established partnership between client and therapist, acceptance for the client by the therapist, and the ability for the therapist to evoke potential change from clients without 'advising' them to make change or telling them what they need to do. Such concepts help form what is known as the 'spirit' of Motivational Interviewing.

Strengths & Limitations of
Motivational Interviewing

Strengths	Limitations
The approach empowers people to take control of their behavior and motivation; client finds their own reasons for change	Therapist must be aware of their own biases; can be unethical if therapist bias influences client
Through active listening & reflective techniques, clients may gain new insight into thoughts & behaviors	Some client situations may require greater education and/or direction from therapist
Is an empirically supported approach and works with diverse populations	MI may not be the best approach for severely mentally ill clients; other modalities may be better suited
MI can help build genuine trust between therapist & client, which allows for greater open dialogue	Therapist must understand and be okay with the non-linear nature of the approach; clients will often slip back into initial behaviors (relapse)
Approach looks to lower resistance and ambivalence; it rolls with resistance instead of fight it	Therapist must avoid jumping into a problem-solving mode and must ensure they are walking with the client and not ahead of the client
Approach is applicable across a wide range of situations or problems	Approach may require a mental shift for some therapists as goal is not to fix a client's problem; this may go contrary to those with a more directive approach
Allows client to feel heard and understood; approach needs clients to discover their own solutions; therapist does not direct	MI sometimes requires more time to establish a genuine trust and understanding between client and therapist as without it, MI will likely not work as well for client

Motivational Interviewing:
The Do & Don'ts

Do	Don't
"Roll with the resistance" and simply listen to the client's fears and problems	Instruct your clients, push them in a direction they do not want, or 'fix' problems for your client
Listen for a client's insights and ideas that hint to what they are willing to do	Become overanxious to get to the "how" part of conversations and try to problem-solve too soon
Collaborate respectfully and brainstorm together without judgement; lead with empathy	Try and motivate a client through coercion, fear or scare tactics
MI and SOC to help conceptualize where a client is at on their journey; such will help conceptualize the case	Use controlling terms like "you must try it, you should do it, you have to, it's better so trust me, do it for me" etc. as it elicits resistance
Find ways to praise the client and affirm their efforts even if there is minimal success; praise the process and not just an outcome	Therapist must avoid jumping too soon into a problem-solving mode and must ensure they are walking with the client and not ahead of the client
Ask about non-compliance to a plan respectfully and without judgement: ask what their understanding of the plan was and for ways the plan can be adjusted	Blame the client for non-compliance to a previously discussed plan and look at non-compliance as failure

"Motivational Interviewing is a collaborative conversation style for strengthening a person's own motivations and commitments towards change..."

THE STAGES OF CHANGE

MAKING CHANGE IS NOT ALWAYS EASY.

Consider the following scenarios:

1. *Bernie is a long-time smoker who does not see it as being an addiction. He does not acknowledge any health concerns regarding his smoking and gets very upset when his friends try and talk to him about it.*

2. *Susan is considering whether it would be of benefit to her overall health and happiness to lose some weight. She thinks about making a nutrition plan but also is not sure whether it is worth doing.*

3. *Bob asked his mom to hire a tutor. His grades have been low and he has decided that he wants to do better. Bob and his mother begin to look up local math tutors in his area.*

4. *Joe is several weeks into his plans for self-improvement, intending to bolster his self-esteem. He steadily attends his therapy sessions, goes to the gym 4-5 times a day, and tracks his diet. He logs his successes in a journal that he fills in daily.*

5. *Sarah has just celebrated her 100th Pilates class at the local workout studio…success! The outlet has been helpful to her both physically and mentally, and she is committed to continuing to improve.*

6. *Kevin was doing well in managing his depression by seeing his counselor and engaging in better life habits. That said, the recent anniversary of his father's death impacted him greatly and he has been in a rut. Kevin stopped attending counseling and stays in bed most of the morning until he has to get up. He is strayed from the plan he created.*

Regardless of the changes a person wants to make, it can take substantial time and consistent effort. It requires a person to assess oneself constantly and to make adjustments—which may be easier said than done because everyone may enter session at a different place in their lives.

THE STAGES OF CHANGE & MOTIVATIONAL INTERVIEWING

Many therapists discuss a concept called "Stages of Change" (SOC) interchangeably with Motivational Interviewing, and which needs to be clarified. Stages of Change is not a technical part of Motivational Interviewing as created by its founders, although they were both conceptualized around the same time. They are not the same thing, but they do work very well together. Because of this, Stages of Change (also commonly referred to as the Transtheoretical Model or the 'Readiness To Change' model) will be discussed here as a resource for anyone wanting to add to their usage of the Motivational Interviewing approach to counseling.

SOC was originally created in 1977 by two theorists, Carlo DiClemente and James Prochaska. They identified five stages through which people will move through on their path toward change. Knowing this model can inform the therapist on how to best approach their client. This model can be incredibly helpful to therapists because they can talk with a client, and based on the discussion, be able to map out which of the stages of change they are at.

Navigating a path to transformation

The five Stages of Change - Precontemplation, Contemplation, Preparation, Action, and Maintenance - serve as a helpful framework for change as it describes a process towards modifying behaviors that could otherwise be confusing or complicated. Armed with this framework, it is possible for a skilled motivational interviewer to tailor their approach and strategy to each of these SOCs.

As was described earlier, Motivational Interviewing is a useful approach to working with an array of people dealing with an array of situations.

MI aligns well with the SOC, which is why they are often discussed together.

When considering true change, it is often that a person will encounter wins and losses, that the path towards growth is not always linear and upward; rather, they will likely experience setbacks. During setbacks, many people can become discouraged and quit on their goals. Understanding these stages and utilizing MI can help a client find new ways to stay motivated as they learn that sustainable change often requires a progression via smaller, well-planned steps.

Let's explore each of these stages:

Stage 1: Precontemplation
In this stage, a person is not really considering change. The person may not be aware of the consequences of continuing with negative behaviors or do not see it as problematic for their life. People in Precontemplation are often described by others as being in denial. For example, a young high school student may be experimenting with drugs. They experience the elevation of being high and feel good when using - all the worries of the world seem to go away. When prompted by the family to stop using, they get mad.

They believe what they are doing is fine and will have no negative outcomes; there is no desire to make a change. In some cases, people in precontemplation may be under-informed about the consequences of negative behaviors.

A typical MI strategy when working with a client in this stage is to focus on the development of a therapeutic alliance while trying not to trigger heightened resistance:

- Create a therapeutic atmosphere of acceptance, positive regard, and compassion - whether you agree with their behaviors or not.
- Be compassionate for the SOC the client is in.
- Trying to move from Precontemplation to Contemplation can be supported by offering factual information about a client's behaviors - and their potential consequences.
  - Such information allows the client to recognize their need to make changes WITHOUT feeling like they were made to or coerced into it.

Stage 2: Contemplation
In the contemplation stage, a client has entered a general understanding that there may be a need for change but might still be experiencing a sense of ambivalence (defined as a state of having mixed feelings and contradictory thoughts about something).

This is an incredibly important phase because many people will never truly move beyond this phase. During this stage, people start to think in a more serious way about the potential benefits of making change, and begin to compare that to the benefits of not making any change. This is where the ambivalence comes into play.

For example, in this stage, a man who has been smoking cigarettes for many years may recognize that there exists some clear benefits to being smoke-free. They are beginning to contemplate life without smoking but also may struggle with the uncertainties of change.

During this stage, the costs of making real change tend to stick out even more, fostering a strong sense of ambivalence. Conflicting emotions can really manifest - all the reasons why a person wants to continue smoking can come up. Doubts and worries can also arise, which may sidetrack the person's desire to really get into the weeds about making change.

This process could keep someone stuck in a contemplation stage for a long while. Some may never move beyond it.

A good therapeutic approach to use when a client is in the contemplation stage is to confirm their entry into a "thinking about it" stage and help them consider a Pro & Con list for making change or not.

- Continuing with the smoking example, a therapist may see all the benefits to change, but they do also need to recognize that from the client's perspective, there do exist benefits to NOT making a change! This needs to be acknowledged.
  - Typically, a person continues within a behavior because some sort of need or positive is being met - even if there are other consequences. For example, a person may continue smoking because it helps them manage stress; this is a positive for them and should be recognized.
  - As a Pro & Con list is created, openly address the ambivalence.
- Help foster a setting of open dialogue without judgment, helping a client work through internal conflicts.
- Therapists should utilize "change-talk" via open-ended questions, which can flush out a client's truest reasons for wanting change.
- An interesting dialogue may focus on the following: What are the pros and cons of staying the same?

Stage 3: Preparation
Entering the preparation stage shows that a client is actively considering making real change and may need support in coming up with plans to do so.

This can be an exciting stage to enter because a client has weighed their pros and cons, and still intends to begin steps towards change.

The therapist should aim to walk with their client as a unified team, working together to develop a plan of action moving forward:
- Begin to develop an achievable action plan - consider taking a larger goal and breaking it down into smaller, manageable parts.
  - All goals, even the smaller steps, should be motivated by a clear sense of intention.
  - Keep the goals realistic and achievable.
- Enhance the client's self-efficiency by boosting coincidence in their ability to change. This can be done by highlighting a client's successes and resources.

Preparation leads to Action.

Stage 4: Action
There is a great deal of important work done in the action stage. Moving between the preparation and action stage, time is spent helping a client move into action by first assessing their readiness to change. The therapist wants to avoid pushing their client into a change they are not wanting to make themselves as such will likely not stick and could cause conflict in the relationship's rapport. Time can be spent exploring the pros and cons of changing or remaining in the status quo, eliciting their personal motivations towards change or no change. Readiness Rulers and follow-up discussions further support the path to action as interventions can be matched up to a client's level of commitment and overall readiness.

Once in the action stage, time can be spent reviewing SMART goals (see upcoming worksheets) while also formulating a realistic and customized action plan. The client must buy into this plan and it should not simply be created by the therapist. Rather, it should be completed as a team.

Time should be spent helping a client both anticipate and overcome potential roadblocks and challenges on their path toward change while also recognizing that the client has resources available to them to help on the quest. Creating a quality plan of action while bolstering a client's own sense of strength and resource can be a great benefit to a client.

As the client moves into action and enacts their personalized action plan, time may be spent reviewing their progress. It will not always be a forward path; there can be setbacks and struggles to take into account. Through all of this, the therapist should continue to:

- Offer the client encouragement and motivation
- Elicit the client's self-evaluation while asking about their progress to date
- Use scaling questions to gauge progress; on a scale from 0 to 10 (low to high), consider asking the client about their progress and overall confidence in the game plan. Be reminded of your OARS:
  - "What have you noticed since you started the action plan?"
  - "What is better? What is different?"
  - "How do you feel about your achievements so far?"

The Action stage usually requires the greatest commitment of energy and time, but is often the stage where a person's change is more noticeable to other people.

Stage 5: Maintenance
The 5th stage of the Transtheoretical Model of Change is referred to as the Maintenance Stage. Here, the client may still be working towards sustained change via their action plan, but they have made notable changes to their behavior. The marker for entering the maintenance stage is usually six months.

As one would expect from both personal or professional experiences, it is not always easy for a person to remain at that stage of maintenance. Sometimes, a person will revert back into their old, hardwired behaviors.

Sustainable change does not end with the action stage as there needs to be a commitment to maintenance. As has already been expressed, MI is not a simple, linear process with a clear starting point and a clear ending point as every client may enter into counseling at a different point in their lives. A person working through the action stage would benefit greatly from continued support from their therapist as behaviors can be embedded and new beneficial habits developed. Without attention to helping a client maintain new behaviors, the potential for a relapse exists.

Eventually, the therapist looks to conclude therapy with their client and terminate/end their professional relationship. Some models of SOC have a sixth stage called Termination. This represents the ending of therapy as the client has maintained the new, positive changes that they have been working on. New habits are embedded and 'have stuck' even in the face of new challenges.

Stages Of CHANGE

01 PRECONTEMPLATION

THE PERSON IS NOT CONSIDERING THE NEED TO MAKE A CHANGE; PERSON MAY BE IN A STATE OF DENIAL

02 CONTEMPLATION

THE PERSON IS ABLE TO CONSIDER THE POTENTIAL FOR CHANGE BUT IS NOT FULLY COMMITTED; THEY EXPERIENCE AMBIVELANCE ABOUT MAKING CHANGE

03 PREPARATION

THE PERSON HAS DECIDED THAT THEY WANT TO MAKE A CHANGE AND BEGIN TO CONSIDER THE WAYS TO DO IT

04 ACTION

THE PERSON HAS MADE SIGNIFICANT STEPS TOWARDS MEETING THEIR GOAL; THEY ARE WORKING TOWARDS THE DESIRED CHANGE IN BEHAVIOR

05 MAINTENANCE

AT THIS POINT, THE PERSON HAS MADE SIGNIFICANT CHANGE; CHANGES ENACTED DURING THE PREVIOUS STAGE HAVE BEEN MAINTAINED SUCCESSFULLY FOR A GOOD DURATION OF TIME

PREPARING FOR

&

ELICITING

CHANGE

WORKSHEETS

The following worksheets can be used by therapists while working within the MI approach to counseling. Some worksheets can be offered to clients as homework and other can be done in session (as a solo activity or one done together, therapist & client).

Most important is the dialogue and conversation that ideally stems from working on some of the activities to come. The magic of MI is found within the discussions and partnership!

As always, it is up to the professionalism and skillset of the therapist to use any and all tools available to them to support their client. Ultimately, it is up to the therapist's discretion how to best use any of the tools or worksheets found in this workbook.

To come will be worksheets designed to help with goal-setting, ways to discuss and work on any encountered ambivalence, measuring a client's readiness to move towards meaningful change, and more.

Preparing For Change
"DARN - CAT"

One foundational skill required to be a good motivational interviewer lies in the ability to ask open-ended questions that invite a client to explore the desire to make change -- otherwise known as Change Talk.

Open-ended questions remain one of the greatest tools in a therapist's arsenal. It may sound like an easy skill to manage but in practice, can be difficult to steadily bring to every session. Quality open-ended questions, when asked properly by the therapist, cannot be answered by the client with a single-word response like 'no' or 'yes' and instead encourage the client to really dive into their thoughts. It is here that Change Talk can occur as it requires thorough reflection.

MI always tries to elicit preparatory talks about potential change. Within the MI world, the acronym "**DARN**" represents preparatory talk about change:

- D (Desire to Change) - "I know that I want to change."
- A (Ability to Make a Change) - "I have what I need to make a change."
- R (Reasons to Change) - "Some reasons I want to change are..."
- N (Need to Change) - "I really need to change because..."

Ultimately, DARN will lead to the acronym of "**CAT**": Commitment, Activation and Taking Steps. If DARN represents preparatory change talk, CAT is all about implementing the change [More on CAT and implementing change will be explored later].

A therapist using an MI-focused lens in session can recognize the change talk that their client is using, which can ultimately help them craft a quality response to their client, with the goal of steering their dialogue toward more action-oriented talk about change.

The following worksheets will look to help explore the inner workings of a person and their true desire for change by exploring goals, personal values and helping a client really consider the potential changes that they may want to make. As is the case for most activities or worksheets, it is possible to work on these tasks together in session or to offer them to a client as a homework assignment to be reviewed for next time. Such a decision is best left to the discretion of the therapist using this workbook and their approach to session.

Either way, it is highly recommended that ample time be spent discussing some of the responses listed on the worksheet, again looking to help a person dig a little deeper. The dialogue, development of rapport and bouncing of ideas back and forth is where the magic happens.

This connection can help a client fully consider their **d**esire for change, potential **a**ctions they can take, the **r**easons and **n**eeds for considering change. This can ultimately encourage a client to shift from preparatory (DARN) change talk to implementation (CAT) change talk.

For example, here are some strategies to consider when discussing the worksheets included here with clients, all while maintaining DARN as a supportive framework:

- Use Open-Ended Questions & Ask for Elaboration: Once change talk is expressed by the client, ask for more detail. Explore using the DARN acronym as a guide.
- Look Forwards with the client: Have a client imagine a future where changes have been made.
- Explore Worst and Best Case Scenarios: Discuss the pros and cons of any potential change / lack of change in an honest way. This will help keep a client from feeling coerced into doing something by the therapist.

Motivational Interviewing:

D.A.R.N Examples

Eliciting "Preparatory Change" Talk

D **Desire to Change**

Therapist Asks: "Why do you want to make this change?"

Client expresses desire to change through words/phrases "I want, I like, I wish…"

For example, "I want to quit drinking."

A **Ability to Change**

Therapist Asks: "How could you do it?"

Client uses the words such as "can, could…"

For example, "I can change. I think I can stay sober."

R **Reasons to Change**

Therapist Asks: "What are good reasons for making a change?"

Client gives their reasons, sometimes using "if…then" statements.

For example, "If I can quit drinking, then I can actually feel better and can be a better parent."

N **Need to Change**

Therapist Asks: "How important to you is it, and why (scale 0-10)?

Client uses the words "need, must, have to, got to…"

For example, "I have got to quit drinking."

Motivational Interviewing:
Change VS Sustain

If Change Talk helps a client towards the direction of making changes, Sustain Talk does the opposite and is more likely to keep a client in the status quo.

According to Miller & Rollnick (2013), it behooves a therapist to recognize sustain talk and change talk when used by clients as it will help better understand and address any of their ambivalence. Clients who are stuck experiencing ambivalence will likely engage in more sustain talk; meanwhile, clients who are more ready and prepared to make changes will begin to make stronger statements supporting change. Change talk and sustain talk represent both polar sides of ambivalence about change. Here are some examples:

Type of Statement	Change	Sustain
Desire	"I want to try and stop drinking so much..."	"I really like drinking..."
Ability	"I think I have the tools and strength needed to quit drinking..."	"I don't really see how I could quit drinking..."
Reason	"If I can quit drinking, then I can actually feel better and can be a better parent."	"Drinking allows me to work through my stress..."
Need	"I need to quit drinking so I can be more attentive to my family..."	"Honestly, I don't even think I need to quit drinking..."

Motivational Interviewing:
C.A.T Examples

Implementing The Change Talk

C   Commitment

Therapist Asks: "What is it that you intend to do?"

Client makes statements about intention and decision; client uses the words/phrases "will, intend, ready, my decision, I am going to..."

For example, "I will quit drinking this week."

A   Activation

Therapist Asks: "What are you ready or willing to do?"

Client statements about their willingness, readiness, planning and preparation.

For example, "I am going attend my first group counseling session tomorrow."

T   Taking Steps

Therapist Asks: "What have you already done? What else can we try?"

Client discusses steps they have already taken; this can lead to further discussion on additional things to try.

For example, "I already threw out all the liquor in my home."

Change Talk allows a client to fully expresses how making a change helpful to them and is truly something they want to do. It helps them consider their ability to do it, the level of committed to, what they need to do or have already begun doing.

Motivational Interviewing:
Change VS Sustain

If Change Talk helps a client towards the direction of making changes, Sustain Talk does the opposite and is more likely to keep a client in the status quo.

Having already looked at DARN, we can now examine CAT.

Change talk and sustain talk represent both polar sides of ambivalence about change. Remember, the therapist needs to actively listen to the client and nurture the change talk while recognizing and working with the sustain talk. Here are some examples:

Type of Statement	Change	Sustain
Commitment	"I am ready to quit drinking & want to begin as soon as possible…"	"I intend to keep drinking and nobody is going to stop me from doing so…"
Activation	"I plan to toss out all the bottles of liquor in my cabinets. I am ready to talk about next steps…"	"I am not ready to quit drinking.."
Taking Steps	"I threw out all the liquor bottles and attending an AA group this week!"	"I went back to the bars this weekend and drank a lot…"

When encountering sustain talk, respond to the client by reflecting back their sustain talk in a non-judgmental. Try to encourage more exploration via open-ended questions. This allows the client to feel heard, that they are not being "talked out of" maintaining a certain behavior.

The Righting Reflex

Recognizing some of the potential challenges to conducting a motivational interview is very important. As was already noted, the 'Righting Reflex' or 'Expert Trap' is one area where a well-meaning therapist can easily fall into a therapeutic approach that functions contrary to the MI approach and overall philosophy. MI is designed to work in partnership while exploring the potential for change; it looks to avoid therapeutic "expert" advice from the therapist.

This "expert trap" (a situation where an assumption or belief that the therapist has the best expert solutions to a client's problems) can accidentally be sprung, contrary to the MI approach to counseling. It is always important for the therapist to remain anchored by the spirit of what MI is looking to do.

What can therapists do to avoid falling into this trap, trying to fix their clients by leading them to the 'right' answers?

- Be an explorer and work in partnership: Go with the client as they explore ambivalence, struggle, pro/cons of working towards change, etc.
- Find time to decrease focus on fixing problems and instead focus some discussion on what it would be like for the client to be living a life closer to their values and core beliefs.
- Evoke discussion of goals, aspirations, personal value systems and other motivators.
- When core values and personal motivators are expressed, consider processing the strategies that have been attempted: what has worked/not worked/worked a little bit/did not work at all.
- Work on reducing the client's need or perceived need to require their therapist to make a change; reduce dependency on an "expert."

Righting Reflex generally comes from a good place, as the therapist is wanting to help guide their client towards an ideal, positive outcome. A therapist can potentially have strong feelings about what behaviors their client should want to change, based on years of academic study and professional experience. In MI, this righting reflex can easily be triggered and the urge to tell clients how they should change can be very real.

When a therapist experiences this urge, it is a sign that they are not in line with the spirit and philosophy of Motivational Interviewing. They need to consider that the client may not have fully embraced this desire for change or may still be clinging to the benefits they feel exist for continuing a behavior (recall the Stages of Change).

The therapist -- armed with education, professional experiences, and their own unique life perspectives -- cannot fully conduct an MI session while automatically thinking that they have all the right answers for another person's life. They are not able to perform this style of counseling while also using phrases like "just do what I am telling you to do, trust me" or "I think you really should...(insert miscellaneous directive)." Such statements are obviously not going to work for this approach.

Another common example of a therapist trying to 'right' or fix a client's situation prematurely is by offering suggestions or solutions without first acquiring the client's ideas and views on a matter. The therapist is not responsible for fixing their client, nor are they responsible for finding the solutions for their client. The therapist taking over the responsibility of finding solutions may potentially weaken client autonomy and self-confidence. This can leave them feeling told what to do, and may even foster a sense of resentment towards the therapist. Such will likely hurt the therapeutic relationship.

Knowing the importance of rapport between therapist and client, the potential pitfalls of the expert trap are significant.

MI requires the therapist to maintain a sense of optimism and hope in the client, an authentic belief that the client has the expertise and capability to bring forth the change they seek. Ideal MI statements or prompts from the therapist may sound similar to the following:

- You are the expert on your life. What ideas do you have?
- I can see how motivated you are to move beyond this setback. What did it require of you to reach this point?
- What characteristics or skills have been the most beneficial to you so far on this journey?
- Can you tell me what you think you'd like to do next?
- What allowed you make it this far and how can I be helpful to you in continuing forwards?

These simple prompts from the therapist empower the client and avoid the therapist simply looking like they already have the 'expert' advice for the client to follow. Instead of trying to fix problems for the client, return to the spirit of MI -- use reflections and brief summaries of what the client is saying. Return to fundamental counseling skills. Hone in on the change talk and process this together, in tandem.

Remember that the goal of this counseling approach is to have the client come up with the solutions as they are the expert within their own life, not the therapist.

This all sounds easier said than done, as falling into the expert trap is something that can potentially occur to a well-meaning therapist. When therapy stalls, when a client experiences a relapse into a previous stage of change, when the client struggles to even see the value in making life change...an understandable instinct to help on the part of a therapist can take over. At the end of the day, the likelihood of a client sustaining a change will directly connect to their motivations and buy-in to the change.

The therapist cannot force or coerce their client to want to change.

If a therapist tries to push their client towards a direction that they are not ready to go, the therapist may be met with resistance and potential resentment.

Often, in wanting to be agreeable, the client will offer a counterstatement like "I hear you, **but**..." or "Yeah, **but**..."

Such can serve as the client's way to challenge the therapist's push. As best described by the work of Fray & Hall in their excellent 2021 book *Motivational Interviewing for Mental Health Clinicians*, working with a client's ambivalence towards change is like pulling on rubber bands: "*The more our righting reflex pulls, the more the person's ambivalence intensifies. Our concern for the person's choice may lead us to persuade, warn, or confront. This stance can rupture the working alliance...instead we work to elicit from the person why they want to make the change, how they might go about doing so...and under what conditions they might commit. When both importance and confidence are strong, people are more likely to move towards readiness.*"

The following pages are designed to be a reflective experience for the therapist (you can write your ideas/thoughts in the open space on the worksheets, or simply reflect on the prompts in your own head). Take the time to reflect on one's approach. Such reflection opportunity will keep a therapist anchored to the principles of this MI counseling approach and will help remind the therapist that they do not need to be in a rush to fix their clients or their problems.

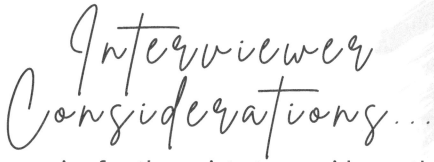

Interviewer Considerations...

This is an exercise for therapists to consider as they begin practicing the Motivational Interviewing approach to working with others. Use the following prompts to consider how well your latest sessions have utilized MI.

Avoiding the Righting Reflex and Expert Trap is a challenge for many therapists. Consider the last time you recognized that collaboration in session had decreased and instead, your 'expertise' and advice was taking over the meeting. What happened?

What were some of the first things you noticed when falling into an expert role instead of serving in a collaborator role? What did you notice about yourself (thoughts, feelings, behaviors)? What did you notice about the client (thoughts, feelings, behaviors)?

What was your comfort level in the expert role instead of the collaborator role? What was the client's response?

What do you think sparked your entry into the Righting Reflex? If you think back, what was going on in session that led to you using a more authoritative session approach?

Consider switching places with the client: How receptive would you be as the client -- listening and following the therapist's directions? If you were the client, what would you be thinking or feeling about the session / therapist / oneself?

What was your intention for taking over the expert role in this session? What were you were trying to achieve (for yourself and the client)?

Enter the Time Machine! Imagine you could go back in time to the session in question. Using the MI approach to counseling, what could you have done better? How would you alter your approach to keep the session more collaborative in nature?

Setting Goals
&
Considering the Future

Goal-setting and considering a desired future can be incredibly important steps for a person when considering whether or not to make significant life changes.

Sometimes, therapists may encounter clients who struggle with finding initial motivation to change or face challenge when it comes to maintaining necessary motivations. Such can hinder a person from living the life they want to live and accomplishing what they want to accomplish.

There are a plethora of reasons why a person may struggle with achieving a goal. One of those reasons may be setting quality goals that are both important enough to chase yet is also achievable. Creating worthless goals that are too easy will not lead to any real sense of fulfillment when completed.

Motivational Interviewing can really support such efforts by exploring want it is that a client really aims to achieve, what benefits would be uncovered by achieving it, and (maybe most important) uncovering what may be holding them back from achieving the goal to date.

The following goal-setting worksheets may be of support in this part of the process. These worksheet have been created to help a client process what they want from their life...and what needs to be done to begin working towards the established goal. Most therapists have heard of the S.M.A.R.T goal concepts - that goals should be Specific, Measurable, Achievable, Realistic and Timed.

Besides SMART goal formulation, Habit Trackers (weekly and monthly) there will be worksheets that allow a client to explore the rewards they hope to earn by accomplishing goals - the "why" behind their desired changes. Additionally, there will be chances to explore core values - this is important because when a client can recognize and embrace their core values, they will be encouraged to accomplish the goals that are in line with such values.

These worksheets can be done by a client on their own and later discussed in session, or they can be completed in tandem. Either way, completing the worksheets are only one part of the process: it is ideal to use these sheets as a springboard into conversation about living a truly fulfilled life.

Helping a person establish a means to tracking their goals can help motivate them while encouraging their desired path towards growth or change. Ideally, some of the worksheets to come that focus on goal setting and tracking can be of benefit.

Creating S.M.A.R.T Goals

COMPLETING CHANGE REQUIRES A PERSON TO MOVE FROM WHERE THEY ARE TO WHERE THEY NEED (OR WANT) TO BE. GOAL SETTING CAN BE MOTIVATING AND HELP THEM MAKE THAT JOURNEY

S	**SPECIFIC** WHAT DO I WANT TO SPECIFICALLY ACCOMPLISH?	
M	**MEASURABLE** HOW WILL I KNOW WHEN IT IS ACCOMPLISHED? HOW IS IT MEASURED?	
A	**ACHIEVABLE** HOW CAN THE GOAL BE ACCOMPLISHED?	
R	**RELEVANT** DOES THIS SEEM WORTHWHILE FOR WHAT I WANT OR NEED?	
T	**TIME BOUND** WHEN CAN I ACCOMPLISH THIS GOAL?	

S.M.A.R.T (R) Goals

Using SMART Goals to help create specific-measureable-achievable-relavent and timed goals is incredibly helpful; creating "smarter" goals (S.m.a.r.t + R) can be next level as it also takes into account motivations and potential rewards.

SMART GOAL

1ST INDICATORS & HINTS OF PROGRESS [MILESTONES & PROGRESSION MARKERS]

REACHING THESE INITIAL INDICATOR OF PROGRESS WOULD DO WHAT FOR YOU [HOW WOULD IT BENEFIT YOU]?

WHAT ARE THE NEXT SMALLER STEPS OR INDICATORS THAT YOU ARE CLOSE TO REACHING YOUR GOALS?

WHAT WOULD HELP YOU CONTINUE TO IMPROVE? WHAT WOULD HELP KEEP YOU MOTIVATED TO REACH THE NEXT MILESTONES?

ULTIMATELY, WHY IS THIS GOAL IMPORTANT? WHAT WOULD BE GAINED IN ACCOMPLISHING THIS GOAL? [REWARDS]

What's My Motivation

Last Name: _____ First Name: _____ Date: _____

What do you hope to accomplish during our conversations together?

In what areas do you what to change, grow, strengthen or improve?

What is the driving force behind you attending counseling session?

Is there anything in your life you could be doing, or want to do, that you can't right now?

When do you feel most satisfied in your life?

When do you feel most dissatisfied in your life?

Habit Tracker

Keeping track of habits and behaviors can help a person stay focused on achieving goals. Place a copy of this tracking worksheet somewhere you will see it each day. Fill out your top 12 daily goals and mark them off each day you successfully complete them. Successful days can quickly build to something much more!

WEEK OF: _____

LIST GOALS BELOW:

	S	M	T	W	T	F	S
01	○	○	○	○	○	○	○
02	○	○	○	○	○	○	○
03	○	○	○	○	○	○	○
04	○	○	○	○	○	○	○
05	○	○	○	○	○	○	○
06	○	○	○	○	○	○	○
07	○	○	○	○	○	○	○
08	○	○	○	○	○	○	○
09	○	○	○	○	○	○	○
10	○	○	○	○	○	○	○
11	○	○	○	○	○	○	○
12	○	○	○	○	○	○	○

Based on the week's progress, do your goals need modification?

_____

_____

Monthly Habit Tracker

Habit	Day

Self-Exploration & Values

One aspect of Motivational Interviewing is understanding that change is not linear and that a person will often go through self-reflection and personal exploration on the journey.

This Self-Exploration & Values Worksheets focuses on a person's core values and desires; it helps a person really spend time reflecting on who they are in the present...and who they want to be in the future, based on what they truly value.

Such an activity can be helpful when a person is challenged by ambivalence, stuck in a place of being unsure about what to do and what they really want or waffling between change talk and sustain talk.

Returning to basics and exploring core values may help them align their values with their actions.

These worksheets are a wonderful activity for both adolescents and adults, applicable in a variety of settings, including individual psychotherapy, school counseling, private coaching, rehabilitation, etc. These activities can also be worked on as a homework assignment or together in session.

When the client has completed the worksheet, it would be wise to facilitate an open dialogue about what the client sees as being their core values and how well their behaviors meet this.

Self-Exploration & Values

Understanding your core values and exploring their importance offers the chance to better know yourself AND what you ultimately want out of life. Take time and really reflect on these questions.

What are the most important things in my life?

If someone asked me what my core values are, what would be my response?

How do I best demonstrate what my core values are?

When and why do I falter from my core values?

How often do my behaviors, or how I live my life, betray (go against) my personal core values?

How do I feel when I act contrary to my ideal core values?

How do you feel when you find yourself acting in a way that positively promotes your personal values?

Are there any areas of your life that you want to change? Are there any changes you may want to make that will better align you with your personal values?

Complete the sentence: "If I was doing a better job of acting in alliance with my core values, people would notice ...?" (What would people notice about you if you acted more in line with your stated values?

Having considered the questions above, what is the likelihood of you wanting to change certain behaviors in order to be more authentically yourself? What would be the first small change you would make?

On a scale of 0-10 (0 being lowest and 10 being highest) How likely are you to want to make some life changes in the coming weeks ahead?

_____

Self-Awareness & What I Value

Read the simple prompts below and fill in the answers using in the blank boxes, putting the first thought that comes to mind. Such can serve as reminder for why a person may be considering change...even when making change can be challenging.

MY NAME IS _____ AND I...

WANT TO...	
AM INSPIRED BY...	
AM DRIVEN BY...	
LOVE TO...	
THINK ABOUT...	
AM HAPPIEST WHEN...	
BELIEVE IN...	
HOPE THAT...	
WILL ONE DAY...	
ONCE TRIED TO...	
WISH THAT...	
AM AFRAID OF...	

ONCE FAILED TO...	
ONCE SUCCESSFULLY TRIED...	
AM DISCOURAGED BY...	
WISH THAT...	
WANT TO SPEND TIME WITH...	
FELT HAPPIEST WHEN...	
BELIEVE IN...	
WOULD TELL MY FUTURE SELF THAT...	
HOPE THAT PEOPLE REMEMBER ME FOR...	
SEE MY BEST QUALITIES AS BEING...	
WOULD LIKE TO IMPROVE...	
WILL IMPROVE MY LIFE STORY BY...	

Agenda Mapping
Helping Calibrate Towards Desired Change

An important strategy for helping clients consider their future is choosing a focus for the time spent together, determining the best way to spend the effort and mental energy. Agenda Mapping can be a great support to the therapist-client tandem when looking to better focus on the work ahead and the overall purpose for spending time together.

This tool allows the client to addresses what their best hopes are for the time spent in session, identifying what they look to accomplish from the counseling experience. Agenda Mapping is most effective when it is based on what the client wants to work on and what they perceive to be most important (rather than what the therapist may think should be the highest priority of the time spent in session).

Sometimes a client will enter into therapy with a very clear direction for what they want help on. For example, a client may be looking return to school and pass their semester classes, to lose weight, quit smoking, achieve a particular athletic training goal, or quit unwanted behaviors like drinking or using drugs.

Other times, the client may enter into therapy without a clear focus. When this occurs, the process of choosing area(s) of focus via agenda mapping is an important next step.

Here's how Agenda Mapping works:
The therapist will offer the client some prompts to help them consider areas for potential exploration and change, based on current and previous conversations between the two.

Agenda Mapping can become even more beneficial when there may exist a general idea of something the client wants to work on.

Imagine this scenario, working with a client who "wants to feel healthier" and wants to "feel better about how they look."

The therapist can fill in some of the bubbles on the Agenda Map, based on the conversations to date. The therapist can ask their client to take a look at the sheet and ask them to consider anything that should be added to the blank bubbles as a possible area of focus. Some bubbles may be very generic and others might be incredibly detailed. The main thing is to allow the client space to write down anything that would fall under the umbrella of "feel healthier" and "feel better about how I look."

Often, the use of the 'bubble sheet' fill-in worksheet for Agenda Mapping can uncovers areas of focus and next steps working together.

The great thing about Agenda Mapping is that it can always be broken down further. For example, the client who "wants to feel healthier" might add comments/bubbles like "sleep better," "spend more time outdoors" and "eat a nutritious meal every morning" onto their map.

Such are some possible subcategories for the mapping of "feel healthier."

Agenda Map: Feel Healthier

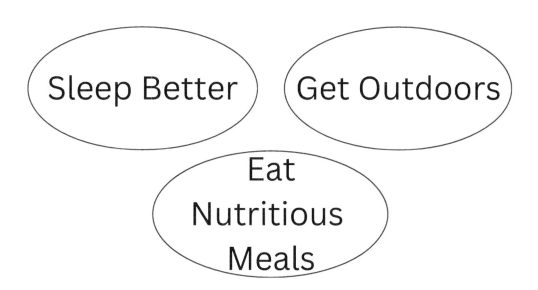

The neat thing about the Agenda Mapping is that it can always be re-explored! Consider the subcategories listed on the previous page - Sleep Better, Get Outdoors and Eat Nutritious Meals can be separate Agenda Maps on their own.

For example, if exploring 'Sleep Better', the tandem might come up with ideas like:

- Create a bedtime routine
- Reduce electronic usage one hour before bed
- Drink a cup of tea before bed
- Finding ways to relax once in bed
- Etc.

From here, with a detailed agenda mapping of 'Sleep Better' created, the therapist can empower their client and help create a strategic direction for the work ahead, simply by asking "what are your thoughts on this agenda map and where would you like to start?"

Finally, the therapist may encourage their client to consider what they deem the most important areas to focus on within the mapping by filling in larger circles/bubbles with what they deem most critical, and lower priority ideas in the smaller circles/bubbles.

The following worksheets can serve as one model of agenda mapping. Ask the client to identify areas of potential focus for the therapist-client tandem to work on together. Have them fill in larger circles with highest priority areas and low priority areas in the smaller circles.

Worksheet 1 will be for a client who has no clear area of focus, allowing them space to write in anything that comes to mind for them.

Worksheet 2 will be for a client who has a general sense of what they want to focus on but may need help in flushing the idea out further.

Agenda Mapping

Please write in any topics we can explore together. Any and all ideas or thoughts are welcome! This can help us determine potential areas to discuss.

Agenda Mapping

Please use this worksheet to further identify some subcategories for your main goal / main area of focus. I might offer a few suggestions and will encourage you to add ideas that you like.

Main Area of Focus: _____

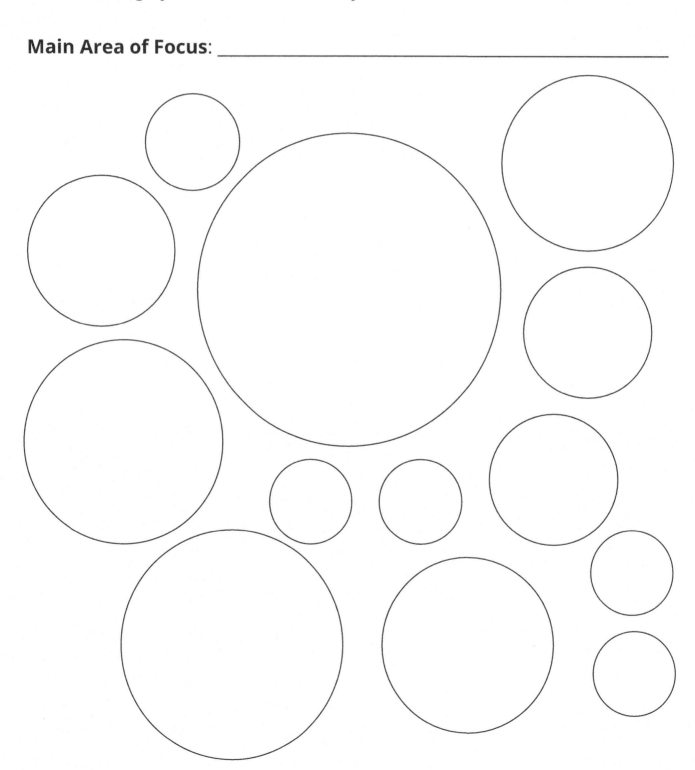

Flashbacks...Flash Forwards

When a person is truly exploring their capability for change, weighing the pros and cons of trying to move from a status quo that has become engrained, it is common for them to get 'stuck.' When a person gets stuck on their own or during a session, using some time to focus on the past can help them reestablish their 'why' for seeking out change.

Discussing the past in a non-judgmental way is an excellent tool in the MI toolbelt, and the Flashbacks worksheet may support these efforts when supported by follow-up discussions to further process and flush out thoughts or ideas.

As is understood in the MI approach, a person will often move between being unsure about change, all the way to wanting an action plan to prepare for change. Discussions about the past and what ultimately led to a person seeking therapy may stoke their fire for more change talk.

Spending time processing the past (hence the name of this worksheet being 'Flashbacks') and giving it some attention can help a client see how past behaviors or actions have affected their life - potentially in both good and detrimental ways. In completing the Flashback worksheet, the client can reflect on their unique past without judgement or without feeling like they are being coerced into making a change that they are not bought into; such may potentially serve as a means to igniting or reigniting their desire to prepare and plan for present change.

Additionally, the Flashforwards worksheet can be used in combination with the Flashback worksheet: once time has been spent processing the past and what led the client to receiving counseling support, time could be spent imaging a world in the short-term and longer term future.

Flashbacks...

Reflecting on the past can often serve as a helpful tool in remembering where we ultimately want to go in the future. Consider the following prompts and jot down the first thoughts or images that come to your mind - no right or wrong. Examine the short-term past as well as a flashback one year previous and see what is uncovered.

I Month Before Session	My Experience
I felt like the best parts of my life were...	
The biggest challenges of my life were...	
I decided to attend counseling sessions because...	
The things I felt most inspired by were...	
The parts of my life that were going the best were...	
The things I needed but did not have were...	
My relationship with friends and colleagues was...	
My relationship with my family was...	
I generally felt like my life was...	

Flashbacks...

Reflecting on the past can often serve as a helpful tool in remembering where we ultimately want to go in the future. Consider the following prompts and jot down the first thoughts or images that come to your mind - no right or wrong. It is possible your life one year ago was a lot different than it is now: flashback and remember what life was like 1 year before attending counseling sessions.

One Year Ago [Before Session]	My Experience
I felt like the best parts of my life were...	
The biggest challenges of my life were...	
I took care of myself by...	
The things I felt most inspired by were...	
The parts of my life that were going the best were...	
The things I needed but did not have were...	
My relationship with friends and colleagues was...	
My relationship with my family was...	
I generally felt like my life was...	

Flash Forwards

Reflecting on the past can often serve as a helpful tool in remembering where we ultimately want to go in the future. Consider the following prompts and jot down the first thoughts or images that come to your mind - no right or wrong. Examine the short-term past as well as a flashback one year previous and see what is uncovered.

5 Years From Today...	My Ideal Experiences
The best parts of my life are...	
The challenges I have overcome are...	
Having overcome many challenges, I now focus on...	
I am proud of myself for...	
Now that my life has changed, I generally feel ...	
The things in life that I value the most are...	
My relationship with friends and colleagues is...	
My relationship with my family is...	
I hope that...	

Decision Balance Tables

A Decision Balance Table can be an incredibly helpful worksheet for a person to complete on their own or with the support of their therapist.

It is important that a client never feels coerced into making a decision about their lives. Motivational Interviewing is a process of walking WITH a client -- not ahead of them or leading them. Lasting change is best accomplished when a person fully explores any ambivalence about making change, has weighed the pros and cons in an honest way, and made their own decision to move forwards. Very often, the therapist will need to quell their own personal opinions on a matter, recognizing the autonomy of their client.

Motivational Interviewing looks to counsel clients with neutrality and a Decision Balance Form demonstrates to the client that you are not coercing them towards YOUR ideal outcome. Instead, the client will analyze the benefits and detriments to making a change or maintaining the status quo.

For example, a client may be considering whether to drop out of school or to remain in school even though the classes have been difficult.

An Decision Balance Table in this example would have four categories of initial focus: Advantages of Changing, Advantages of Status Quo, Disadvantages of Changing, Disadvantages of Status Quo.

- Advantages of staying in school / Advantages of leaving school
- Disadvantages of staying in school / Disadvantages of leaving school

The intention is to have the therapist/client tandem work together in considering each category equally and openly.

Such will yield a great deal of conversation together.

Decision-Balance Tables

Write the ADVANTAGES and DISADVANTAGES for making change. Fully flush out the pros and cons! The results will give you a new perspective on the situation/event.

Advantages of making the change (list potential change)	Advantages of maintaining the status quo (list everything)

Disadvantages of making the change (list potential change)	Disadvantages of the status quo (list potential change)

The Making Changes Scale

Do My Behaviors & Values Match-Up?

The Making Changes Scale Worksheet can serve as another tool or method to allow a client opportunity to explore the benefits and detriments to making change or maintaining status quo.

This worksheet can support a client in considering their behaviors, values of importance, and whether the behaviors and values are in accordance with each other or contradictory to each other.

For example, if a parent values being a mother or father to their child but has behaviors that cause them to not be a good parent, this can create some internal struggle.

If a teen loves their parents and wants to honor them, yet disobeys their requests to go to school and complete homework, dissonance may be experienced.

It can be important for a person to really consider if the values that they *say* they hold actually match up to their actions.

Offering this worksheet for a client to complete and then process together may serve as an excellent tool within motivational interviewing. Discrepancy between reported values and actions can expose potential dissonance and may even lead to more change talk.

The Making Changes Scales

Please fill in the following survey to explore whether the changes you are considering match up to the values hold. Below, write down the goal that you are considering. Then, fill in the remaining survey questions!

	Not Important at All (1)	Neutral	Incredibly Important (5)
How important is it to you to make this change?			
How confident are you that you could make this change?			
Would making this change make you feel better about yourself?			
How important is it to you that you make this change as soon as possible?			
How much do the thoughts and feelings of other people in your life influence your desire to make a change?			

In what ways does your current behavior conflict with your personal values?

Does your current behavior conflict with any of your personal goals?

The Two Roads...

Motivational Interviewing and Stages of Change both demonstrate within their framework that the process of making change is not always a simple decision, a Yes or No. A person will often move throughout those pre-contemplation/contemplation phases before deciding to actually move towards the formulation of gameplan an actionable path towards the desired change.

The Two Roads can help a client visualize where they are at on this journey through making change. Some of the questioning on this worksheet will combine the spirit behind Stages of Change as well as the spirit of "DARN" from Motivational Interviewing.

How a therapist ultimately decides to use this worksheet is up to them and their expertise; that said, it is recommended that this sheet be used as a supportive tool when a client is spending time in the contemplation stage. This worksheet can serve as a visual representation of the conversations that the therapist and client have had discussing the benefits and detriments to committing to making change.

An integral part of this entire process is being able to have a client openly consider any existing ambivalence and their reasons for and against making change. The Two Roads Worksheet may help with this, leading the therapist/client tandem into worthy conversation. As has already been said, making the decision to change is not an easy one. The process of evoking means utilizing change talk to help the client fully flush out their reasons for wanting change. Armed with such, they can make the best decisions for themselves.

The purpose of this worksheet is to use the "fork in the road" imagery to encourage the client to consider where they are at and what the potential outcomes would be if they took a particular road.

What do they see for themselves on the road ahead?
How close to them is the fork (making the decision to change or maintain status quo)?
Why do they want to make this change?
Why are they motivated to do this work?

This worksheet can also help the therapist gain a better understanding of where the client is at in terms of stage of change. Knowing where a person is at in terms of SOC can inform the discussions to come.

The Two Roads...

Imagine that you are walking on a long, empty highway. As you peer ahead, you notice that there is a break in the road, a fork ahead.

This imagery represents the potential for change that you have been thinking about and/or discussing. The road forking to the left represents the path towards change; the road to the right is the path if you stay the same. The road leading up to the fork represents how close you are to making the actual change.

Mark where you are currently at on this path.
Once marked, fill in the blank prompts on the front and back.

Making Change

Staying
the
Same

How close are you to the fork in the road/making a decision?

Consider where you marked yourself on the road. What made you mark the spot that you did? Why did you not mark yourself further back?

Thought Exercise: What would it look like if you took the path towards the left? What will life look like one year from now if you took this path?

Thought Exercise: What would it look like if you took the path towards the right? What will life look like one year from now if you took this path?

Imagine Yourself 5 years from now. What advice or suggestion would 'Future You' tell 'Current You' ?

Becoming the Hero of Your Story

One interesting and potentially thought-provoking activity can be the Create Your Own Character worksheets. Such worksheets can be useful for all different types of people and ages as it will require the person to take a very positive, optimistic view of their lives and potential for change.

Often, people can be pessimistic on their own ability to change or grow for the better. There can be resistance to moving into a new world where the status quo that has been lived will change; there can be legitimate, conflicting feelings about moving through the SOCs, or maybe a person has struggled through the SOCs previously...only to fall back and relapse into a pattern they once tried to leave.

The purpose of this activity is to inspire the client into recognizing their own agency, resource and opportunity -- the ability to define the person they want to be, the HERO of their own unique story.

Ideally, by this point in the therapeutic relationship, there has been time to address any existing ambivalence through an open and honest discussion. In such discussions, the intention is to put the power for change in the client's hands.

Let the client create their own unique hero - one that is based on having achieved all the goals and feats they aspired to. Such an activity may allow the client to imagine a life beyond ambivalence and into change beyond their status quo.

The therapist should consider their client's personality when offering this worksheet and follow-up discussions as "superhero" conversations may not be for everyone. That said, this activity can help someone begin to at least imagine a world where they are in control - the heroic figure of their own lives.

Create Your Heroic Character

Time to get Super & Amazing by creating **yourself** as a superhero -- one who is like you in every way...with some creative flare added to the profile. Additionally, imagine that this character has accomplished all the growth and change they aspired to achieve. Who is this character? What do they stand for? What do they believe? What do they hope to achieve? How do they inspire others?

What is your heroic superhero name? What is your important catch-phrase or motto?

Character Descriptions

What gifts and powers does your hero have? How did they gain these unique gifts or traits?

Heroic Feats

What gifts and powers do you as a superhero have? How did you gain these unique gifts or traits?

Character Lore

What is the greatest challenge you as the superhero has overcome?

Villains on the Attack

Every hero has a villain - and every villain looks to exploit a weakness in the hero's armor. What weaknesses would you as a superhero have?

Heroic Feats

Some superheroes stand for truth and justice while others look to be the friendly neighborhood protector. What is it about the future heroic YOU can be inspiring to other people?

Behaviors on Trial

Motivational Interviewing works on the principle that lasting change becomes possible when a person has made the commitment to change instead of having an expert tell them that they should make a change. It is designed to strengthen a person's self-motivation by exploring their own internal arguments for change.

Within MI, a person often will put their own behaviors and reasons for change "on trial."

MI respects that both the therapist and the client have expertise and experience to draw from - that the sharing of information is to be considered a collaborative effort that is in response to what the client is saying during session. The therapist's expertise is used to try and evoke change talk while working through sustain talk; the style is not designed for a therapist to simply tell their client what to do.

As cliché as it may sound, the biggest step in the process of making a lasting change is in WANTING to make it for oneself. This is where the Spirit of MI comes into play (the key elements collaboration, evoking and working to draw out the client's own ideas about change).

Behaviors on Trial

Analyze whether or not making a change would be of benefit to you and what would be different if you maintained status quo.

The Potential Change on Trial:

If I make the change, the most noticeable changes to my career / school / professional life would be...?	
If I make the change, the noticeable changes to my important relationships (friends, family, colleagues) would be...?	
If I make the change, how would I feel about myself? What would I notice is different?	
If I do not make the change, what would be the most noticeable consequence to my career / school / professional life?	
If I do not make the change, what would be the most noticeable consequences to my most important relationships?	
If I do not make the change, how would I feel about myself? What would I notice?	

What would be the BEST case scenario to the career / school / professional life if I make the change?	
What would be the BEST case scenario for important relationships (friends, family, colleagues) if I make the change?	
What would be the long term implications if I was to make the change?	
What would be the WORST case scenario to the career / school / professional life if I make the change?	
What would be the WORST case scenario for important relationships (friends, family, colleagues) if I make the change?	
What would be the long term implications if I was to NOT make the change?	

The Verdict? _____

_____

Planning to Succeed

One of the most important steps in making true behavioral change is in the formulation of a plan that is designed to succeed. Without a good, efficient plan, the likelihood of failure is increased.

This worksheet works very well with a client who is moving beyond contemplating whether to make a change or not, and has decided to get into the weeds, discuss details to a plan and enter into the step of preparation.

It is important to prepare for success by not rushing through this critical step; the quickest way to deflate any positive momentum is to have a plan be rushed, highly flawed, and ultimately fail. Larger problems needs to be attacked in smaller steps, allowing for the change to experience some victories and conjure up momentum.

Most important is to make sure the goals are the client's goals, and not goals established by the therapist. If a person is not really invested in a particular goal, the likelihood of them sticking with it during tougher times is lessened.

The reality that setbacks could arise needs to be discussed...and plans for this inevitability should be considered as well! For example, if working with a student who wants to improve his grades, simply deciding 'to do better' is not enough!

Planning to Succeed

What is the behavior that I want to change?

What would change for me if I was to stop doing the undesired behavior?

What steps do I need to take to make these changes happen?

- _____
- _____
- _____
- _____

How will I know if I am making progress towards my goals?

- _____
- _____
- _____
- _____

What is my ultimate motivation to change?

What are the potential roadblocks to me completing my desired goals?

1

2

3

Notes:

What should I do if I start to fall backwards, away from desired goals?

1

2

3

Notes:

Describe your life once you complete all your goals. What fears or insecurities did you overcome?

Daily Journaling & Self-Reflection

Helping Track Actions & Motivations

One of the most important steps in making true behavioral change is in the formulation of a plan that is designed to succeed. Without a good, efficient plan, the likelihood of failure is increased.

This worksheet works very well with a client who is moving beyond contemplating whether to make a change or not, and has decided to get into the weeds, discuss details to a plan and enter into the step of preparation.

It is important to prepare for success by not rushing through this critical step; the quickest way to deflate any positive momentum is to have a plan be rushed, highly flawed, and ultimately fail. Larger problems needs to be attacked in smaller steps, allowing for the change to experience some victories and conjure up momentum.

Most important is to make sure the goals are the client's goals, and not goals established by the therapist. If a person is not really invested in a particular goal, the likelihood of them sticking with it during tougher times is lessened.

The reality that setbacks could arise needs to be discussed...and plans for this inevitability should be considered as well! For example, if working with a student who wants to improve his grades, simply deciding 'to do better' is not enough!

Daily Self-Reflection

Mood/Emotion Tracker

◯ ◯ ◯ ◯ ◯

LOW MOTIVATION ⟷ HIGH MOTIVATION

What were my main goals & intentions for today?

What went well for me today:

I am Appreciative For:

Reflections on the day:

What I accomplished today to get me closer to where I want to be:

The Readiness Ruler

It can be common for a person to enter into therapeutic session and have a variety of concerns they wish to discuss. Within these concerns, that same person could be in a variety of places in terms of their readiness to address it. As is understood with Motivational Interviewing, it is a therapist's job to

For example, imagine beginning to work with a person who enters into session wanting to discuss areas of his life that he hopes to feel better about:

- He says that he is considering whether it would be good or not to apply for a new job. There are aspects to the current job he enjoys but wonders if it would be better to look for something different.
- He knows he wants to get in better health and stop smoking so much marijuana. He has thought about it for a long time and wants to try and find a way to create a plan he can stick with instead of quit like all his past attempts at finding better health habits.
- During initial discussion, the client also shares that he drinks "almost every single day" but that it is not an area of concern for him right now. When the therapist asked a clarification question, he responded back that he doesn't want to talk about it.

When using an MI lens to consider this client, there could be a lot to work with and several areas to discuss. Ultimately, it is recommended that the therapist really hone in on a focus for session while also considering where a person is in terms of their readiness to discuss change.

Using SOC as a tool looking at client-readiness for change, it appears that he is precontemplation for any drinking/alcohol issues (he drinks almost every single day but does not want to talk about it), is in a contemplation phase in terms of considering his occupation, and is working through a contemplation/planning phase in terms of finding better health habits.

As was initially taught by MI founders Miller and Rollnick, this approach advises the therapist to engage with their client as a teammate and equal partner on the journey. Therapists do not lead the session and tell the client what to do, refrain from unsolicited advice / directing and look to avoid confrontation.

Instead, MI helps people examine their own unique life situations, discover what they really value, rally the intrinsic motivation to change behaviors and create a plan towards the desired outcome.

The Readiness Ruler Worksheet helps gauge where a client is on addressing the concerns they bring up in session. In the example given, a client who uses the Readiness Ruler may then recognize that they really do want to get healthier. Congruently, if they were to fill out a ruler on the area of daily alcohol consumption, it would likely show a low desire to change (based on them being in the precontemplation stage).

Think of Motivational Interviewing to be like driving a car: In some approaches, the therapist is the expert in the room and thus it is up to them to drive the car, provide the fuel, and navigate an ideal course. In MI, the therapist is not driving and instead is supporting their client from the passenger seat, serving as a helpful and attentive passenger while the client steers from the driver seat.

Use this tool to help a client consider what they really want to accomplish and how ready they are to go after it.

The Readiness Ruler

Consider the areas of your life that have motivated you to seek out counseling. Pick out one of these areas and write it in below - then, answer the questions that follow by simply putting a checkmark on the rating scale. The Readiness Ruler may help in identifying your readiness for real change while also exploring any ambivalence or roadblock to beginning the process.

RATING SCALE: 1 = LOW DESIRE OR SCORE / 5 = HIGHEST DESIRE OR SCORE

QUESTIONS:	RATING SCALE (1 – 5 SCALE)				
	1	2	3	4	5
One area of my life that I am thinking about making change in is ... (write in a potential change you may want to initiate within your life):					
On a scale of 1 to 5, how difficult was it to come up with a behavior you wanted to consider making a change within? (1 = Not too difficult / 5 = Incredibly difficult)	○	○	○	○	○
How important to you is this change?	○	○	○	○	○
How ready are you to actually do what it takes and start making changes?	○	○	○	○	○
How confident are you that you will be able to change behaviors, meet my goals, and come closer to being who you want to be?	○	○	○	○	○
How likely are you to begin taking steps towards meeting this goal within the next 14 days?	○	○	○	○	○
How likely is it that 30 days from now, you will have lost motivation and will have stopped trying to make change? (1 = low likelihood / 5 = incredibly likely)	○	○	○	○	○
How urgent is it to you to make change to this behavior or habits?	○	○	○	○	○
How realistic is it that you will be able to make significant change to behaviors and replace it with something else that benefits you or makes you happier?	○	○	○	○	○
Considering all the above questions, how committed are you to beginning the process towards change, sticking with it during tougher times, and ultimately completing the mission?	○	○	○	○	○

Relapse Planning

Motivational Interviewing, as has already been discussed, can be used in a variety of ways, within many different settings, for a wide range of client issues. A client will not always just continue to move forwards and improve; any experienced counselor knows that the people they work with will often slip backwards. Within the MI model, such is almost to be expected and prepared for by the therapist.

The general meaning of a relapse in terms of the transtheoretical model is when a person falls back to a previous stage on the SOC model after an improvement.

For example, imagine a woman who had created the goal to become healthier by cooking more meals at home, eating one helping of veggies each dinnertime meal, working out 4 times a week, and throwing away all processed candies: Once deciding to make a change, creating a customized plan for herself and doing it for a short duration ... she fell into an emotional rut and stopped everything she was once doing. She fell back into the contemplation stage, wondering if it was even worth while to try and make these big changes; "I wonder if I would just be happier eating whatever I want..."

Such would qualify as a relapse as she fell out of the action SOC and reverted back into the contemplation SOC.

The term 'relapse' is most often used in terms of addiction, alcoholism and drug use. Inside the world of addiction to drugs or alcoholism, a relapse is a return to substance use after a period of nonuse and abuse. MI is a fantastic approach when supporting a person working though addiction as it focuses on connection to a client and the importance of aligning while remaining non-judgmental. The supportive therapist will recognize that people will often need to move through stages of change.

Relapse occurs often within addiction recovery and is considered a natural part of the process towards making sustainable change. People who attempt to make genuine change or look to overcome addiction may experience relapse before finding the success they seek. Sometimes people will cycle through the SOCs several times along their journey towards change!

The therapist should consider that some clients may think that a 'slip' backwards or a full relapse is a definitive sign of failure. Some clients might even consider abandoning the goals they set and quit on themselves. The therapist can use the rapport developed and the qualify of their conversation to encourage them to get back to work and try again.

Be it for addiction issues, or really anything else, it would be worthy conversation for the therapist and client tandem to consider a relapse prevention plan, which is modeled on the worksheet to come. Again, the client can work on this in session or on their own; that said, it is always recommended that ample time be spent processing the prevention plan in an open way.

One prevention planning form will be generalized and the other will be more specific towards addictions to substances as discussed above. There will also be a form that helps a client identify specific triggers that may predict a relapse. If time is spent recognizing potential roadblocks and planning for them, it may help should those challenging triggers actually show up.

Relapse Prevention Planning

Famous boxer Mike Tyson once said that "Everyone has a plan until they get hit." Discussing a plan for preventing relapse can be of great benefit. Examining potential roadblocks can help us be better prepared for when they arrive.

What is the goal or outcome you have been working towards?

List what inspired you to make goals and plan for change (why are you here)	
List some potential triggers or roadblocks that could lead to you pulling back from your goals.	
Who can you talk to when struggling to maintain on a path towards your goals?	
What message can you tell yourself when struggling to meet your goals or action plan?	
List how life will look different if you were to revert back to previous behaviors	
List how life will look different if you were to maintain your action plan and sustain a path towards change	

Relapse Prevention Planning

For Drugs / Alcohol / Substance Abuse

Famous boxer Mike Tyson once said that "Everyone has a plan until they get hit."
Discussing a plan for preventing relapse can be of great benefit.

List some activities or skills you can use when thinking about using.	
List some potential triggers or roadblocks that could lead to you using.	
Who can you talk to when struggling to maintain on a path towards your goals?	
What message can you tell yourself when feeling the urge or desire to use again?	
List potential outcomes and consequences of a relapse.	
List potential outcomes for maintaining a path towards sobriety.	

Relapse Prevention Planning
The Cheat Sheet

MY GOAL	MY 'WHY'	MY MOTIVATIONAL MANTRA

WHO DO I HAVE ON MY TEAM? WHO CAN I CONTACT FOR SUPPORT?

RESOURCES AVAILABLE TO ME

ACTION STEPS [WHAT TO DO WHEN I FEEL LIKE USING]

WHAT CAN I DO IN THE SHORT-TERM TO GET MY MIND OFF OF USING RIGHT NOW?

Relapse Prevention Planning
Recognizing the Triggers

This worksheet will help identify and plan for any potential triggers that can arise. It is common for someone working towards significant life changes to fall backwards into previous behaviors, even when still desiring change. Time here will be spent identifying and focusing on those triggers that can negatively influence our current behaviors, thoughts and motivations.

What is the main change you are looking to make in your life?

Below, consider potential triggers that may arise for you in each given category.

People or Places	
Activities or Situation	
Thoughts I Have & Emotional States I Experience	
Things	
Miscellaneous Other Triggers	

Consider the list you completed on the first part of this worksheet. Describe your biggest potential triggers (place, people, situations, your emotional state, etc.) in order below:

Trigger #1	
Trigger#2	
Trigger #3	

Now, consider each trigger and let's gameplan. What can you do to either avoid each trigger or at least minimize it's effect on you?

Trigger #1	
Trigger#2	
Trigger #3	

Session Evaluation Form

Please consider each statement and ponder how it applies to you. There is no right or wrong questions - just please answer honestly. Some questions will ask you to offer a score of 0 (low score) to 10 (highest score). Be sure to include any comments or thoughts in the comment section.

Overall, I rate my session today a score of _____ What went well in today's session?

What was the most helpful or supportive aspect of today's conversation?

The therapist was welcoming, attentive, and was inclusive of my experience and perspective during the session _____

We spent time discussing what I wanted to discuss _____

During my next session, I might want to discuss...

Therapist : Self - Evaluation Form

When practicing a therapeutic tool like MI, it can behoove the therapist to take time and reflect on their session. As part of a journal or self-reflection tool, the therapist can print out several copies of this form and fill it out immediately after an MI session. This can help document new improvements while also allowing space to consider where more growth is required.

Overall, I rate my session today a score of _____ What went well in today's session?

What MI - related skills did I use well today?

What MI - related skills do I need to improve upon, based on my session today?

How receptive to the MI approach was my client?

During my next session, one MI - related skill or approach I want to better utilize is...?

QUICK GUIDE

DESK REFERENCE

&

RESOURCES

SUPPORTIVE DESK GUIDE

1 What is Motivational Interviewing?

MI is an empirically researched, efficient strategy that uses client motivation and therapist / client rapport to work towards change - a client-centered approach.

2 Why Use the MI Strategies?

MI works when a person makes their own decision to change instead of being told what to do; it is their idea as the therapist does not tell a client what to do.

3 When to Use MI?

Best to be used when a person is stuck and not progressing - time to try something different. Change words are an indication that they are moving past ambivalence.

4 Listen for Change Words

Listen for change words or phrases that demonstrate that the client is contemplating change: includes things like I want, I think I can, I will, etc.

5 The Benefit of Rapport

MI is an empirically researched, efficient strategy that uses client motivation and therapist rapport to work towards change; a truly client centered approach

6 The Questions to Ask in MI

Why do you want to do this?
Why is it important to you?
What steps can you take right now?
What do you see improving for you?
Discuss discrepancy between goals / values and behaviors.

7 Use Your 'OARS'

Remember the 4 Steps to OARS
-Open-Ended
-Affirmations
-Reflections
-Summaries

8 Reflection & Summaries

Mirror what the client says and work in collaboration. Summarize to link together key relevant information as it can serve as a nice connection or bridge between topics.

MI Processes & OARS

1 ENGAGE

Remain Client-Centered / Person - Centered in approach. Do not try and 'fix' the problem for the person

2 FOCUS

Focus on areas that are important to the client; priority is the client's autonomy and needs

3 EVOKING

Elicit and explore the client's motivations, goals, personal values and resources; use abilities and skills to move towards an ideal change

4 PLANNING

Planning serves as the pathway to change; work with client on a plan that they adopt and buy into

---

Open-Ended Q's

Q's that cannot be answered w/ Yes or No

Invites the client to open and share; rely on active listening and genuine curiosity

"Can you tell me more about…?"
"What would happen next…?"
"Clarify what you mean when you said…"

Affirmations

Authenticity and congruence is important; Therapist should aim to be sincere in recognizing the client successes or motivations

"It says a lot about your care as a father that you are wanting to make this change…"

Reflections

Offers the chance for therapist to show they are listening; helps create collaborative space

Mirror what the client says in session

"From what I hear you saying…"
"It seems like…"
"Wow, that must be…"

Summaries

Further demo's to client that therapist is listening and understanding

Tie together all relevant info into a concise summation; Client can hear back their story and responses, ambivalence and motivation

"Ok, let me make sure I understand…"

Stages of Change & Strategies

1 Precontemplation

There is no active thought to make a change; person does not see behaviors as being problematic enough to make a change.

2 Contemplation

Person is beginning to think that there is a need to make a change; there is consideration for making a change.

3 Preparation

Person has made the decision / commitment to change within a reasonably short amount of time

4 Action

The person is already taking action and making behavioral changes

5 Maintenance

The person has been sustaining changes made for 6+ months; person is bought into sustaining their new lifestyle

6 Relapse

A regression to an earlier stage occurs; a failure to maintain the existing position in SOC model

General Mindset & Strategy

Precontemplation: Focus on developing relationship with the client and being genuinely curious about the life of the client; explore the client's perspective and views on their behaviors. Discuss with client the potential risks regarding the status quo.

Contemplation: Try to reduce sustain talk; have client explore what could make their situations better or worse; explore what life could look like with change.

Preparation: Return to discussions on goals and make plans for achieving those goals. Develop an action plan with client to organize available resources, develop strategies.

Action: Elicit discussions with the client that are focused on times of success and what might work moving forwards; troubleshoot roadblocks; encourage & reinforce client.

Maintenance: Continue to encourage the client on maintaining their plans towards sustained change; continue to offer genuine praise and recognition for the client sustaining their changes successfully for a healthy duration.

Relapse: ID the triggers that led to a relapse and inability to maintain the action plan; eventually look to re-establish commitment; begin progressing through each stage again.

Motivational Interviewing
Sample Questions

Intro Questions & Rapport Building

- What brings you here today?
- What ultimately inspired you to schedule a meeting with me today?
- Is this the first time you have met with a counselor before?
- How did it feel after you scheduled our session?
- What is your ultimate hope for our time together?
- What do you expect from the overall counseling process?
- What are some wishes or hopes you have for yourself that could come from our being successful working together?
- What do you do that makes you feel happiest and fulfilled?
- What are some of your favorite things about yourself?
- What are some of your hobbies?
- Who is most important to you in your life?
- What is the best compliment you have ever received?
- If your house was on fire and burning down, what is the first thing you would grab and secure, and why?
- What would be the title of your autobiography?
- How do you think you are perceived by others?
- Who are some of your real life heroes and inspirations?
- How do you feel talking with me, a stranger, about your life?
- What do you see being some of the benefits of having someone to talk about life with?
- Is there anything that you are uncomfortable talking about with me?
- What are the positive outcomes that can come from our time together, if things were to work out well?
- Would you feel comfortable spending some time working together and talking about your life?
- So where should we begin...?

Motivational Interviewing
Sample Questions

The Potential For Change & Ambivalence

- Where are you at, in terms of wanting to make a change?
- What are some of the pros and cons of making this change?
- How do you feel right now, discussing this potential for change?
- Tell me about what has inspired you to consider making such a change?
- What is happening in your life that is making you want to make such changes?
- Let's take some time and explore the potential benefits of making a significant life change.
- Have you tried to think about what your life would look like one month after deciding to make this change?
  - One year from now? Five years from now?
- Have you tried to think about your life if you do not make the change one month from now?
- What would your life look like if you chose not to make a change and continue the status quo?
  - One year from now? Five years from now?
- When you consider making a change or remaining with the status quo, how do you feel?
- Are you feeling split in any way?
- What do you think is causing any ambivalence?
- Let's take some time and explore any potential drawbacks or detriments to making this change.
- What are some of the negative outcomes to trying to make change?
- When considering change, what are the main factors that will contribute to your decisions?
- What do you value the most in your life and how will such influence your decisions to change or remain within the status quo?

Motivational Interviewing
Sample Questions

The Challenge of Making Change & Inspiring Client Resiliency

- When it comes to making a significant change, what do you see as the biggest support factors available to you?
- What personality traits do you have that can indicate your ability to make this change?
- Have you ever had to make significant life changes before?
- Can you share a time where you faced a similar challenge?
- On a scale of 1-10, how confident are you that this change can be made?
- What allows that score to be that high?
- What would it take to move your score one point higher on the scale?
- Can you share a previous experience in your life where you overcame a challenge and sustained the desired changes?
- What did you learn from that experience?
- What does it mean to be resilient?
- What does it say about you that you were able to overcome challenges and make significant change?
- To be successful in making these new changes, are there new supports, resources or skills that will be needed?
- How much do the people in your life play a part in your desire to make change?
- What would your most trusted friend or family member say to you?
- What strategies have you used in the past to maintain your motivation?
- Have you ever tried to make this change before and if so, how might you go about this challenge differently?
- What skills or supports are needed to help ensure your path towards making and sustaining the desired changes?

Motivational Interviewing
Sample Questions

Aligning Goals and Values

- What is most important to you in life?
- What do you value the most?
- Do your current behaviors or actions align with those values?
- Along with your values, what do you see as being your most important duties or priorities?
- How does making this change fit with those priorities?
- When your actions and behaviors match up and align with your values, how do you tend to feel about yourself? Life?
- When your actions and behaviors are contrary to your values, how do you tend to feel about yourself? Life?
- How would your life look different if you were successful in making a change?
- What are your long-term goals or aspirations?
- What are some shorter-term goals that can build towards those longer term aspirations?
- Would making this change help you towards reaching any of those goals?
- Does the current status quo align with what truly matters to you?
- When you reflect on your life, what are you most proud of?
- If you were to reflect on your life 10 years from now, what would you want that future-life to look like?
    - What would you want to have accomplished or experienced?
    - What would be the same as today? Different than today?
- How does the potential for change fit into that image of you 10 years from now?
- What would it do for you to finally commit to a plan that would lead you to the lifestyle and future you say that you ultimately want?

Motivational Interviewing
Sample Questions

The Commitment Towards Change

- Having spent some time discussing your strengths and resources, how do you feel about now making the plans needed to accomplish the change that you want?
- What would be the first, small step towards realizing the ultimate change you want to complete?
- What are some concrete steps you can take towards making change?
- What are some shorter-term goals that can help build towards larger goals?
- Is it possible to break down the path towards change into smaller steps that would make it more likely to find some initial 'wins?'
- What are some smaller steps to take that can increase your confidence?
- If we were to meet one week from now, and it was a successful week for you, what would have occurred?
- If you were to accomplish some of these smaller steps, what do you think you would notice about yourself?
- What might other people around you notice?
- Let's commit to the first step and smaller, short-term goal that you want to complete this week.
- What are some potential roadblocks or challenges in the process?
- What roadblocks can come up for you this week?
- Knowing and recognizing these potential roadblocks, what are some strategies you can use when facing such challenge?
  - How will you maintain your motivation and commitment?
  - Can you make a commitment to yourself - a commitment on what to do if you encounter a roadblock?
- What other challenges can potentially come up for you?
- As change is not always easy to accomplish, what can you do to manage any stress or emotional struggle that may come up?
- What is your ideal self-care plan for the week?

- What mantra can you create and use for yourself while being successful going through your plan?
- What mantra can you create and use for yourself when being faced with a roadblock or potential for falling back/relapse?
- What do you tell yourself if you want to quit?
- Having spent time already discussing your strengths and available resources, how can you involve them this week?
  - How can your network of friends and family support and motivate you?
  - How can I help you?
- Have you ever tried to track your daily successes?
- What can you do to help track your successes?
- If you were to achieve some of your steps towards ultimate change, what will you do to recognize this milestone?

Motivational Interviewing
Sample Questions

The potential for relapse into a previous stage of change (or previous undesired behaviors) is highly likely when working with clients, especially those managing substance abuse concerns. The greatest gift MI can offer those clients is empathy by lending an ear to what mindset or attitude could be interfering with any established plans or goals. MI can reframe the relapse as a learning experience instead of something to be shameful of. Returning to discussions about the motivation for change, the benefits and costs for potential change, and a person's unique resources (strengths, characteristics, supports, etc.) would be ideal next steps. Discussing such factors in collaboration will foster the therapeutic relationship, strengthening rapport. Using open ended questions can help the tandem explore the relapse in a nonjudgmental way. Then, discussions on next steps can occur.

- What happened? (open up discussion of the relapse and it's prelude)
- How were you feeling leading into the relapse?
- What happened right before the relapse?
- At what point did you recognize that the potential of slipping backwards was possible?
  - What were some of the changes you noticed?
  - What was different about this situation?
  - What were some of the thoughts you had before relapsing?
- What did you do to try and avoid slipping into undesired behaviors?
- Looking back, what could you have done to try and avoid the relapse?
- How are you feeling about everything now?
- If you imagined your immediate future (insert a time frame - one week, one month, one year, etc.), what will it look like if you stay on this trajectory?
- What are some ideas you have to reignite your motivation and get back on your desired track?

A Final Word...
(and a Thank You)

Thank You for taking the time to consider the Motivational Interviewing approach to counseling and some of the ideas included within this workbook. Whether you offer these worksheets to clients or use these worksheets to fuel dialogue, I sincerely hope some of the ideas help you in your practice.

The single best counseling advice I ever received was from a supervising clinician who would always give her supervisees reflective activities designed to foster empathy with our clients.

"Opening oneself to therapy is a truly courageous act," she would say.

One reflective activity she offered her supervisees required the therapist to imagine interviewing their client one year after termination. The client has promised to be completely, 100% genuine and honest with you.

- What would the client say about the time spent with you in session?
- What would the client say about their experience with you in therapy?
- Would they reflect positively or negatively about the experience?
- Would the client feel like you pushed them towards YOUR desired outcome or would they express feeling like you worked together in partnership?
- Did they feel supported and understood within the sessions?
- Frankly -- did they like working with you (why or why not)?

Being able to place yourself in the shoes of your client demonstrates the ability to empathize. The more you consider the counseling experience from the view of the client, the greater your ability to empathize and partner with clients will be.

References/ For Further Exploration / Suggested Research

TO MAKE IT EASIER TO NAVIGATE THIS WORKBOOK, I INTENTIONALLY AVOIDED HEAVY DISCUSSION ON RESEARCH AND REFERENCES TO OTHER PRACTITIONER'S WORK. THE FOCUS WAS ON OFFERING THE GENERAL INFORMATION KNOWN IN THE COUNSELING WORLD ABOUT MOTIVATIONAL INTERVIEWING AND PROVIDING SOME WORKSHEETS THAT COULD BE USED AS A TOOL TOWARDS STIMULATING WORTHY DISCUSSIONS BETWEEN THERAPIST AND CLIENT. EVERY THERAPIST IS ARMED WITH THEIR OWN UNIQUE TOOLBELT FULL OF STRATEGIES AND INTERVENTIONS THAT ARE BASED ON CONCEPTS DISCUSSED BY PRACTITIONERS BEFORE US, IN ONE WAY OR ANOTHER, TO VARYING DEGREES. IN UNDERSTANDING THIS, HERE ARE SOME INTERESTING RESOURCES ONE MAY WISH TO EXPLORE FURTHER TO DEEPEN THEIR KNOWLEDGE OF MOTIVATIONAL INTERVIEWING. ULTIMATELY, IT IS UP TO EACH THERAPIST TO EXAMINE THE WORK AND PERSPECTIVE OF OTHERS AND EQUIP THOSE TOOLS THEY FEEL ARE OF BENEFIT, WHILE LEAVING TOOLS THAT ARE NOT AS HELPFUL ON THE BENCH.

MILLER, W.R. & ROLLNICK, S. (1995). WHAT IS MOTIVATIONAL INTERVIEWING? BEHAVIOURAL AND COGNITIVE PSYCHOTHERAPY, 23(4), 325–334. HTTPS://DOI.ORG/10.1017/S135246580001643X

MILLER W.R, ROLLNICK S. (2002). MOTIVATIONAL INTERVIEWING. PREPARING PEOPLE FOR CHANGE. 2ND EDN. NEW YORK: THE GUILFORD PRESS, 2002.

MILLER, W.R., ROLLNICK, S. (2013). MOTIVATIONAL INTERVIEWING: HELPING PEOPLE CHANGE, 3RD EDITION. NEW YORK: THE GUIFORD PRESS, 2013.

DREW, C. (2023). MOTIVATIONAL INTERVIEWING QUESTIONS EXAMPLES (2023). HELPFUL PROFESSOR. HTTPS://HELPFULPROFESSOR.COM/MOTIVATIONAL-INTERVIEWING-QUESTIONS-EXAMPLES/

FREY, J., & HALL, A. (2021). MOTIVATIONAL INTERVIEWING FOR MENTAL HEALTH CLINICIANS: A TOOLKIT FOR SKILLS ENHANCEMENT.

GUENZEL N, MCCHARGUE D. ADDICTION RELAPSE PREVENTION. IN: STATPEARLS [INTERNET]. TREASURE ISLAND (FL): STATPEARLS PUBLISHING.

HAQUE, S. F., & D'SOUZA, A. (2019). MOTIVATIONAL INTERVIEWING: THE RULES, PACE, AND OARS. CURRENT PSYCHIATRY, 18(1), 27+. HTTPS://LINK.GALE.COM/APPS/DOC/A572716209/AONE U=ANON~600A3DC7&SID=GOOGLESCHOLAR&XID=914F619F

KREMER, J., MORAN, A.P., & KEARNEY, C.J. (2019). PURE SPORT PRACTICAL SPORT PSYCHOLOGY. LONDON: ROUTLEDGE.

VOWELL, C., PHD. (2023). WHAT IS MOTIVATIONAL INTERVIEWING? A THEORY OF CHANGE. POSITIVEPSYCHOLOGY.COM. HTTPS://POSITIVEPSYCHOLOGY.COM/MOTIVATIONAL-INTERVIEWING-THEORY/

SUBSTANCE ABUSE AND MENTAL HEALTH SERVICES ADMINISTRATION. (2021). USING MOTIVATIONAL INTERVIEWING IN SUBSTANCE USE DISORDER TREATMENT. ADVISORY.

SUBSTANCE ABUSE AND MENTAL HEALTH SERVICES ADMINISTRATION (US). (2019). CHAPTER 3—MOTIVATIONAL INTERVIEWING AS A COUNSELING STYLE. ENHANCING MOTIVATION FOR CHANGE IN SUBSTANCE USE DISORDER TREATMENT - NCBI BOOKSHELF. HTTPS://WWW.NCBI.NLM.NIH.GOV/BOOKS/NBK571068/

"

The mediocre teacher tells.

The good teacher explains.

The superior teacher demonstrates.

The great teacher inspires.

"

WILLIAM A. WARD

Printed in Great Britain
by Amazon

56571585R00071